RELIGIOUS BUILDINGS

By the Editors of Architectural Record

RELIGIOUS BUILDINGS

AN ARCHITECTURAL RECORD BOOK

McGraw-Hill Book Company

New York	Paris	London
St. Louis	São Paulo	Madrid
San Francisco	Singapore	Mexico
Auckland	Sydney	Montreal
Bogotá	Tokyo	New Delhi
Düsseldorf	Toronto	Panama

CREDITS

The editors for this book were Jeremy Robinson and Patricia Markert. The designer was Patricia Barnes Werner. The production supervisors were Elizabeth Dineen and Sara L. Fliess. It was set by The Clarinda Company and printed and bound by Halliday Lithograph.

The introduction to Chapter One was excerpted from a building type study editorial by Elisabeth Kendall Thompson.

Library of Congress Cataloging in Publication Data
Main entry under title:
RELIGIOUS BUILDINGS

Religious buildings.

"An Architectural record book."

1. Churches — United States. 2. Synagogues — United States. 3. Architecture, Modern — 20th century — United States. I. Architectural record.
NA5212.R44   726'.0973   78-27106
ISBN 0-07-002342-5

1234567890   HDHD   7865432109

ARCHITECTURAL RECORD SERIES

Affordable Houses
The Architectural Record Book of Vacation Houses, 2/e
Buildings for Commerce and Industry
Buildings for the Arts
Campus Planning and Design
Great Houses for View Sites, Beach Sites, Sites in the Woods, Meadow
   Sites, Small Sites, Sloping Sites, Steep Sites, and Flat Sites
Hospitals and Health Care Facilities, 2/e
Houses Architects Design for Themselves
Houses of the West
Interior Spaces Designed by Architects
Office Building Design, 2/e
Places for People: Hotels, Motels, Restaurants, Bars, Clubs,
   Community Recreation Facilities, Camps, Parks, Plazas, Playgrounds
Recycling Buildings: Renovations, Remodelings, Restorations and Reuses
Religious Buildings
Techniques of Successful Practice, 2/e
A Treasury of Contemporary Houses

ARCHITECTURAL RECORD SERIES BOOKS

Ayers: Specifications for Architecture, Engineering, and Construction
Feldman: Building Design for Maintainability
Heery: Time, Cost, and Architecture
Heimsath: Behavioral Architecture
Hopf: Designer's Guide to OSHA
Portman and Barnett: The Architect as Developer
Redstone: The New Downtowns

Table of Contents

INTRODUCTION

This book presents the most current architecture, including renovations, designed for religious use, that has appeared in *Architectural Record* over the past twelve years. These buildings represent a wide variety of denominations, from Katselas's solution for a renovation of a monastery to Otani's design for a highly specialized religious sect's headquarters. There is a design for a Unitarian suburban church, for an Orthodox synagogue in the city, for a Reform temple on Long Island, for two missions in tropical climates, and for a modern cathedral in San Francisco.

Over-all, besides the variety of buildings and design approaches, there can be found some common design concerns among these structures. One common problem that the architect confronts is scale—how does a religious building relate to its surrounding environment? Some blend into the fabric of the neighboring community and landscape (Lafayette Orinda United Presbyterian Church, p. 130); others stand out as landmarks, easily recognized for their special purpose (St. Francis de Sales Church, p. 116). The Charles River Park Synagogue (p. 148), recessed and sheltered from the urban area in which it is situated, leads you step by step through a series of walls from the busy street outside to the quiet dignity inside. Stanley Tigerman, in his design for St. Benedict's Abbey (p. 88), conceals most of that structure underground, leaving the impression of diminished scale between the roof and the rest of the building. In a few cases, the buildings call attention to their massive structures and are meant to have a large scale in relation to the individual participant, to the entire congregation, and to the community at large (St. Mary's Cathedral p. 92). These large structures, along with the more modest-sized ones, do not recall so much the traditional monumental cathedral or basilica. They do impress one, though, with their dignity and elegance, characteristics inherent in all religious architecture, regardless of its scale.

The buildings collected in this book also share a certain simplicity and directness of expression in their designs for the contemporary user. The interiors remain relatively simple, without too much decoration, focusing the congregation's attention on the bema, the altar, the pulpit, the chancel. In contrast to the elaborate detail and intricate artwork of St.

Thomas Church (p. 152) in New York, one of the older churches in the book, St. Thomas Aquinas Church in Indianapolis (p. 52), in its simple design, guides the eye of the participant directly to the altar, without any decoration blocking the path. This concern for focus within the church or temple has always dominated religious architecture, but in most of these buildings it is demonstrated in a new, dynamic, sometimes dramatic, way. It could be in a design feature such as toplighting (Congregation Beth Torah, p. 54), or arrangement of seating (St. Peter Claver, p. 64), or the radial pattern of firs in the ceiling above the sanctuary (Northwoods Presbyterian Church, p. 80).

Since today's religious building gets used more than one day of the week, the architect is prompted to design his program with the day-to-day needs of the community in mind. The adaptability of space, which is given an entire chapter, stands out as another feature shaped by many of the projects on the following pages. An emphasis on secular and religious functions of the community ensures that the building will be used, that the neighborhood is aware of its usefulness, and in a way, guarantees the longevity of the building itself. When we see the Tuskegee Chapel (p. 104) being used for both religious services and musical concerts, or the First Christian Church (p. 8) set up for as wide a range of activities as church services, bingo games, and day care center, we know that these buildings are serving their communities to the maximum capacity.

A note on the organization—the chapters are not meant to be rigidly defined. Some of the projects in one chapter can easily fall into another. The article on the monastery at Belmont Abbey (p. 43) examines the architect's response to both renovating a structure and providing for the specific needs of a religious community. In the same way, several of the buildings in the sixth and seventh chapters examine not only how a building fits into its specific site, but also how it is suited for flexibility of space.

Whether visually exciting or serene, relying on old forms or creating new ones, these buildings give an idea of what direction religious architecture is taking and the many problems an architect must face, as well as the many solutions possible when designing religious buildings.

CHAPTER ONE:

FLEXIBLE SPACE IN RELIGIOUS BUILDINGS

Perhaps the most penetrating question of all, to the architect, who must deal with the program, and to church member and contributor, for whom the economics of church building are inescapable, is, "Why should the church building be used only one day out of seven?" We can only offer a few clues to the answers of these and other questions about the use of religious buildings. For one thing, although church buildings have continued to be built at a fairly steady rate, that rate is nowhere near the rate of the sixties. And this has induced considerable reappraisal of purpose, mission, and need.

The church buildings constructed since the mid-sixties have been unlike traditional church buildings—not because building committees, or architects, or both, were striving for a fashionable contemporary architectural expression or searching for a means of making a strong image, but because these buildings resulted directly from the particular needs of the people of the church. Thus people—not liturgy, or unidirectional function, or structure—have become the major influence on the design, form, and plan of an increasing number of church buildings.

Simplicity, directness, relevance to needs, flexibility, and adaptability—these are the design goals of the building programs for new church structures today. And of these goals, flexibility is the most important. Whatever space is built must have flexibility, must be usable for secular activities as well as for religious functions, and must not be the characterless "facility" so many multipurpose places have been in the past. Economics has been a major factor in this new requirement, of course; but common sense about idle space cannot be ignored in understanding this new approach to use of religious buildings.

To design multi-use space which works well, and is as appropriate for social occasions as for church services, is a challenge—of a different order from ringing one's own changes on Gothic or Colonial, but just as difficult, if not more so, to solve satisfactorily. The church buildings shown on the following pages show in what ways some architects have taken the challenge, and have derived programs directly from the needs of the people they serve.

Church of Our Divine Saviour

The Church of our Divine Savior in Chico, California, is designed as a "place of encounter," for the individual with groups of people in ritual and social situations. Every provision of the plan answers a requirement of an encounter: the chapel, tabernacle and garden are quiet places for meditation; confessional and counseling office are for face-to-face talk; at the baptistery, a small group can gather, and can flow in to the main space or out to the garden, or be cut off from activities in the rest of the building. Small groups can meet in the lounge; for informal occasions with chair, lectern and table removed, large groups can meet, dance or play games in the main space. With sanctuary furniture in place—in *whatever* place is appropriate to the occasion and the group size—as many as 370 can attend mass in the same space. The main space can become two spaces without losing its identity; the two spaces can become one without losing their identity. One part of the main space is architecturally defined by four columns and an inclined plane which acts as an interior "roof" but is open to the skylight of the main space. When divided, this main space can provide space on one side for 200 people in an informal activity and on the other for 200 people gathered around the table at mass. Without ostentation, this church, like many others of today, emphasizes people and their needs, and it becomes, in an area of trailer parks and small homes, a landmark of importance and a focus of neighborhood activities. The building is air-conditioned.

CHURCH OF OUR DIVINE SAVIOR, Chico, California. Architects: *Patrick J. Quinn and Francis Oda*. Engineers: *McCain & Associates* (structural); *Belden & Wistort* (mechanical/electrical). Contractor: *Novak Construction Co.*

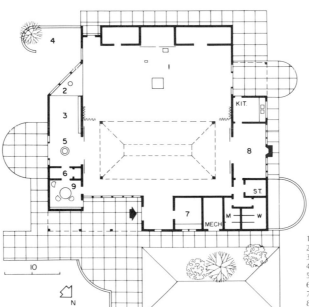

1. Movable altar, lectern, seat
2. Tabernacle
3. Meditation Chapel
4. Meditation Garden
5. Baptismal Font
6. Confessional
7. Sacristy
8. Lounge
9. Office

While design for Our Divine Savior Church was still in preliminary form, The Guild for Religious Architecture gave it one of its annual awards commenting, however, that "while the congregation's seating should be movable, there seems no reason why the altar should be too." Today it is the unmovable altar (and all other unmovable sanctuary furniture) that is more likely to be questioned. The award recognized the degree of flexibility designed into the main space, as the photographs show: (top) traditional nave sanctuary relationship, with seats for 160 (or more if seats are placed on three sides of the altar; (center) seating for 300 around the altar, filling the whole space; and (bottom and opposite page) simultaneous use of the main space, here divided for two kinds of activity (worship in one, meeting in the other), and two areas at the sides. The chapel at left for meditation, the lounge for a small study group.

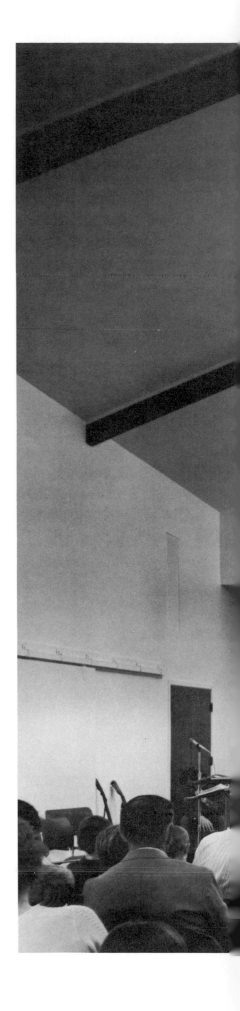

Church of the Blessed Sacrament

An emphasis on people, not structure, and on space that adjusts to church functions instead of the function having to adjust to the space, led to the totally flexible nave and sanctuary of the Church of the Blessed Sacrament in East Hartford, Connecticut. Only two elements in this interior space are fixed: the circular 25-seat chapel and the sacristy-storage-kitchen-lavatory unit, both freestanding and located near the entrance so as to form, between them, a narthex. All sanctuary furniture is movable—the 500 chairs are stackable, the altar, ambo, seat and font can all be stored—so that the character of the open nave can be completely changed as its use for other than religious services changes. This space is used for a variety of purposes, all related to the church program and varying from parish business meetings to social functions. For smaller group meetings, the narthex becomes a meeting room. The structure is simple: nine columns support an exposed space frame, all elements of which are painted white. Light fixtures are suspended within the space frame, and banners, tapestries and other pieces of art hang from it, adding bright colors to the white walls. The simple, almost plain exterior, faced with vertical cedar boards painted white, is surprisingly in scale—considering the volume of space enclosed—with the surrounding neighborhood.

CHURCH OF THE BLESSED SACRAMENT, East Hartford, Connecticut. Architects: *Russell Gibson von Dohlen Inc.*—*John L. Riley,* partner-in-charge of design; *Allen P. Tracy,* structural design; *Ralph H. Gibson, Jr.,* acoustics. Engineers: *Peter Dalton & Associates* (mechanical/electrical). Landscape architects: *Maine & Associates.* Consultant: *Russell Vacanti of Vision in Design, liturgical appointments.* Contractor: *The Hall & Fiske Company.*

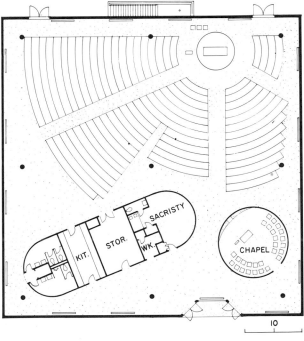

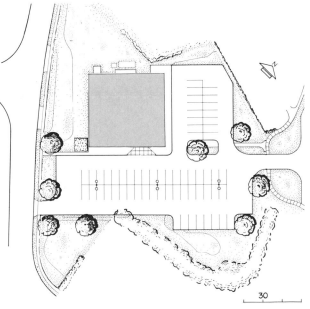

The all-white nave is important in creating the character of the interior. The red carpet throughout the interior is the only permanent color in the building, since the colorful banners and other art work suspended from the space frame can be moved. When furnishings are moved and stored for special events, the character of the interior is completely changed, but with the required fittings for religious service in place, the dignity and serenity of a church is re-established. The small circular chapel at the entrance, however, is a permanent religious space, with fixed furnishings. In it is kept the reserved sacrament, and it is the place where daily and memorial masses are said. Its white stained walls are 12 feet high, and open at the top. The narthex is used for baptisms and meetings.

First Christian Church

Kirksville, Missouri is a town of 15,000 people about 200 miles from St. Louis. Like most small regional centers, its churches are an active part of community life; not only are there services and Sunday school, but pancake suppers, day care centers, Boy Scout meetings—and maybe even bingo games. The building of the new First Christian Church on these pages was an important event, and the architects—Anselevicius/Rupe/Associates—quite naturally describe their design as a dialogue with the community as a whole. They have also dealt creatively with the special liturgy of the church itself.

The bell tower (photo, right) is intended as a new landmark in the city, drawing people to it and placed on the most active corner of the site. It is turned at a slight angle to help "enclose" the raised court on which it is placed, and the court is the main entrance-way to the church. The exterior of the church is simple and residential in scale, to match that of the neighborhood around it. There are no spectacular forms outside; in fact, the whole design is focused inward to preserve its good neighborliness and respond to the active and noisy streets on two of its boundaries.

The entrance vestibule is low, with natural brick and soft browns to act in contrast to the main focus of the design, the sanctuary itself (opposite page). Here daylight streams in, the roof appears to float above the congregation, and the curved brick wall tries to avoid setting limits to the space. Anselevicius/Rupe have said the curved wall is one way of bringing the congregation in closer communion with themselves and with their minister, while still following a basically basilican plan. The brick walls of the sanctuary are painted white as a further suggestion of unlimited space and inclusiveness.

In the Christian Church, each new member of the congregation is wholly immersed as a part of the baptismal ceremony, and the architects here have made that part of the liturgy an architectural event. Immersion takes place within the sanctuary, not behind it as in many Christian churches, and in the center of the chancel space. The people to be baptized first walk down into the baptismal pool using the corridor behind the chancel, then out into the sanctuary through special doors behind the altar (see page 9).

Plants have been set on the congregation side of the pool. (Photo, opposite.)

The subsidiary spaces of the new church expand the usefulness of the whole property. The major side aisle of the sanctuary has windows looking out on a garden, which will become a quiet and sheltered court yard when the future administration wing is built (see site plan). The sanctuary can be opened to the outside from this wall. The older education building is still in use on the site, and can be reached directly from the rear of the church. A coat room and a lavatory are located adjacent to the narthex, and can be converted into a bride's room by sliding doors. The choir has a dressing space near the rear of the church, and the choir loft is above the narthex within the sanctuary. The new church is a quiet building in its small-scaled neighborhood setting, meeting the complicated functional and emotional needs of the community it serves.

FIRST CHRISTIAN CHURCH, Kirksville, Missouri. Architects: *Anselevicius/Rupe/Associates.—Charles R. Nash, project architect.* Structural engineers: *Thatcher and Patient, Inc.;* mechanical and electrical engineers: *Londe-Parker;* contractor: *Irvinbilt Co.*

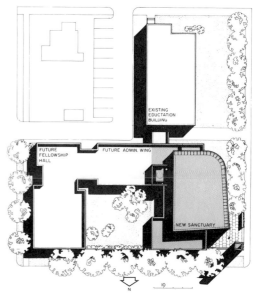

Robert Pettus photos

The photo (top, left) is a side view of the First Christian Church in Kirksville, showing the area of the open court which will be created when future expansion takes place (as in the site plan at left). The skylight running around the major curved face of the sanctuary is also visible in the photo (above, left) and is an important architectural feature. It admits brilliant daylight (above) and is visible as a kind of "crown" to the church at night. It is made of acrylic plastic in anodized aluminum mullions, and one face of the skylight is frosted. Materials for the church as a whole are dark brown face brick·outside and on many surfaces inside, except the sanctuary, which is brick painted white. Ceilings are painted drywall and floors are concrete, with carpeting.

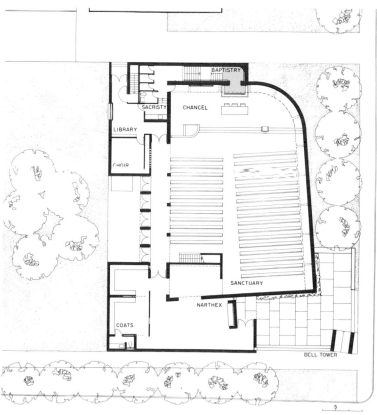

The baptismal pool is placed behind the altar, and a white cross set in relief on the white brick wall completes the simple furniture of the chancel. When the baptismal pool is in use, the two doors (which help form a dramatic circle in the wall when closed) are opened to reveal the brick archway into the pool. The inside of these doors is painted a bright blue to match the blue behind the archway, forming a surprising new pattern on the white wall, as in the photo above.

A street in front of the church (photo, left) contrasts with the serenity of the interior.

Frank Lotz Miller photos

Floor plan labels: STOR. / STOR. / AREA 2 / KIT / PATIO / STOR. & SOCIAL AREA / STOR. & GAME RM / AREA 1 / SANCTUARY / ORGAN / CRY ROOM / CHAPEL / CONF. / SHRINE

St. Patrick's Catholic Church

The program for this Roman Catholic church called for a great deal of flexibility for round-the-week use, and it had as well to make a visible impression to tourists on the nearby highway leading to Alabama Gulf Coast beaches not too far away. Three specially divisible areas were required, and they are achieved in the plan which is shown above: a permanent chapel which can seat up to 80 people, a secondary seating area to bring the seating capacity to 250 on Sundays, and a third area which could be used for church services but could also be adapted to secular activities. The building can be used for one, two, and three separate functions simultaneously, or combined into one room for large and special services. Most of the architectural emphasis here, then, is on a special set of church functions; for the rest, the building is for the most part extraordinarily simple and dignified, sitting quietly on its site in a grove of tall pine trees. Four separate roofs pitch upward towards the central area, which corresponds to the central crossing in churches of traditional design.

ST. PATRICK'S CATHOLIC CHURCH, Robertsdale, Alabama. Architects: *J. Buchanan Blitch and Associates—J. Buchanan Blitch, Bill Argus, Jr., and Eduardo Camacho.* Engineers: *D. E. Britt and Associates (structural); J.V. Reuter, Jr., (mechanical); Schroeder and Associates (electrical).* Consultant: *Sean Cullen (furnishings and stained glass).* General contractor: *D. and A. Equipment Company.*

Church of the Brethren

The Church of the Brethren in the rural community of Live Oak, California, is designed for full-time use, meeting community as well as church needs. On weekdays the major spaces of the building are used as a child care center, a facility that the town lacked and desperately needed, and that the church wanted to provide as part of its program of community service. In the evening the building is used for a variety of other activities, both church and community-oriented. The new building replaces an earlier Carpenter Gothic structure on a small lot which could not accommodate an expanded program of activities. Although the program for the new building premised a multi-use space rather than a specifically designed meeting room, the Building Council members had a clear idea of the character that they wanted this principal space to have when they wrote: "It must be a simple place of beauty for worship . . . a warm enfolding room but at the same time durable and able to withstand the wear and tear of many uses." A difficult and challenging assignment, but achieved here in plan and design. The high, open, natural-lighted main space, with vistas to patio and play garden, has the required character, and with sliding panels on all four sides, is adaptable for privacy and size.

CHURCH OF THE BRETHREN, Live Oak, California. Architects: *Dutcher, George and Hanf.* Engineers: *Goplen & Yokoyama* (structural/foundation); *Marion, Cerbatos and Tomasi* (mechanical/electrical). Consultants: *Bolt Beranek & Newman Inc.* (acoustical), *Fred D. Pitman* (architectural representative, Department of Architectural Services, American Baptist Extension Corporation). Landscape architects: *Dutcher, George and Hanf.* Contractor: *Lamon Construction Co. Inc.*

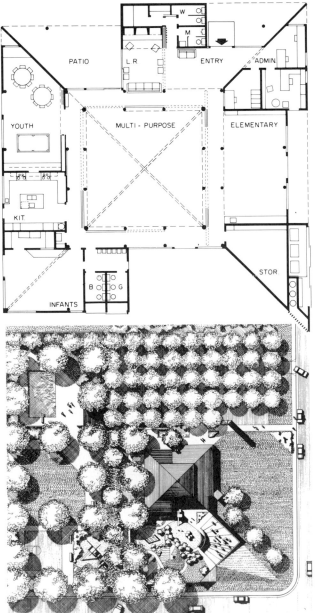

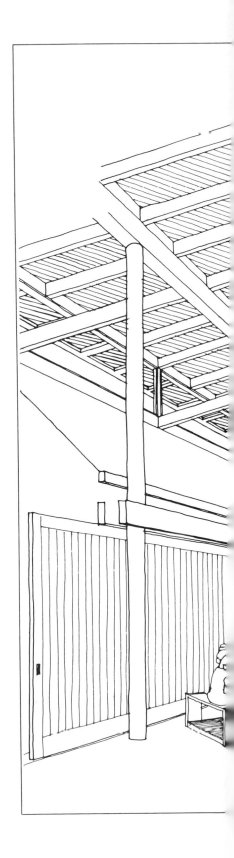

Temple Beth-El

At the heart of the program for this Long Island Reform synagogue addition was the requirement that the new sanctuary function equally well for small daily congregations, bar mitzvahs and weddings, and for overflow congregations on High Holy Days. From a practical point of view, this meant anywhere from a few dozen worshippers up to 1900 or more. Architects Armand Bartos & Associates studied this requirement carefully and responded with a scheme that not only accommodates various numbers easily but vigorously expresses the various uses of this flexible space.

The components of the sanctuary are permanent main floor seating in two sections—one in a diagonal relationship to the bema, balcony seating above (including a projected section extending down to the main floor), and temporary seating under the balcony and in the social hall which may be opened through a sliding partition to become part of the main space. The front aisle of the balcony continues around the whole space, unifying it by providing the visual ligament that links all its elements. Also providing unity is a broad, suspended ceiling that follows the pattern of the pews below and conceals lighting fixtures and air conditioning supply ducts. Between the suspended ceiling and roof structure, over the bema, Bartos has introduced a canted skylight that brings daylight down to highlight the ceremonial area. A matching skylight (photo right) illuminates the rear wall of the balcony and aids in giving the whole sanctuary a clear spatial definition.

The building is framed in steel; dressed in brick. Interior walls are finished in white, textured plaster. Seats are upholstered and aisles are carpeted. Both the pews and the suspended ceiling are light oak. The total effect is lively but disciplined, quietly luxurious—at least in terms of its detailing and level of finish—but not in the least pretentious.

TEMPLE BETH-EL, Great Neck, New York. Architects: *Armand Bartos & Associates—Armand Bartos, partner-in-charge; Roy Friedberg, project manager; Martin Price (partner until May 1973), project designer.* Engineers: *Lev Zetlin Associates* (structural); *Flack & Kurtz* (mechanical/electrical). Sculptress: *Louise Nevelson.*

Norman McGrath photos

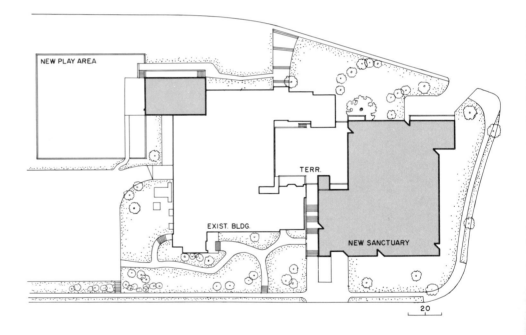

NEW PLAY AREA

TERR.

EXIST. BLDG.

NEW SANCTUARY

20

Main entrance is reached from the street by a stair set between the existing building and the new sanctuary. The visitor enters through a low vestibule (photo left) into a spatially exciting main reception space enlivened overhead by stairs leading to balcony seating. Photo (opposite) describes the relationship between inside and out. Skylight, at rear of balcony, illuminates the main avenue of circulation.

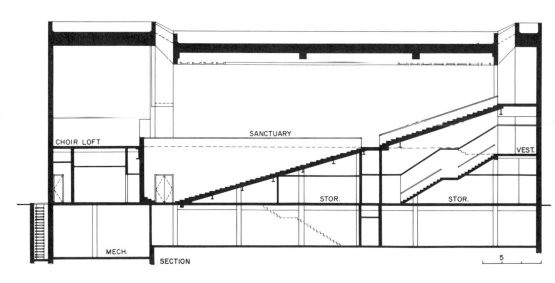

CHOIR LOFT · SANCTUARY · VEST.

STOR. · STOR.

MECH. · SECTION · 5

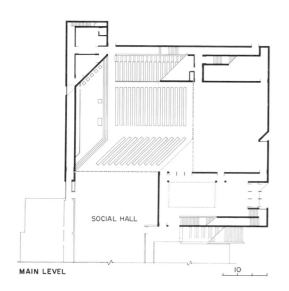

SOCIAL HALL

MAIN LEVEL

10

BALCONY LEVEL

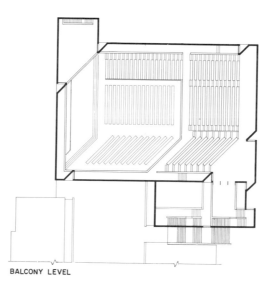

Flexibility is clearly expressed in the plans. Permanent seating includes 392 on the main floor, 133 in the diagonal side section and 364 in the balcony. In addition, a movable partition under the balcony may be opened to provide 370 temporary seats. When overflow crowds are anticipated, the social hall may also be opened to provide 620 more temporary seats, giving a grand total of 1900. All are within 100 feet of the bema and have unobstructed sight lines to the ark and pulpit.

Lionel Freedman photos

First Unitarian Church

It was quickly apparent when the Church building committee met with its architect that what was wanted was no ordinary church. Sensitive to the changing nature of religious instruction and worship itself, the committee wanted a structure that would act as a community focus all week long. The program that emerged from these discussions was admittedly experimental. It called for a large meeting room supported by a series of spaces that are inviting for uses not directly related to worship but keyed to the congregation's social and creative values. The result (see plan) is a series of open-plan studios for painting, ceramics, wood working, sewing, and similar pursuits. On weekends, these studios are to be used for small-group religious instruction. These spaces open to a common, landscaped court so the functions can spill outdoors when the weather is appropriate. The large meeting room, used Sundays as a sanctuary, can double during the week as a space where the community can gather for concerts or discussions.

The general character of the building finishes will be informal and the structure itself scaled to the surrounding residential community.

Architects: *Ulrich Franzen and Associates*—associate in charge: *Allen Anderson*. Structural engineers: *Aaron Garfinkel & Associates;* mechanical engineers: *Benjamin & Zicherman*.

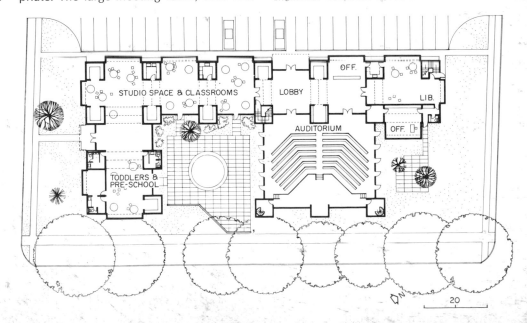

Views of the bema and the tensile-steel-roof structure through the walls that enclose the sanctuary help to create a sense of continuity in surrounding spaces, when these spaces are used for overflow seating during High Holy Days. Planting, planned for the skylit corridors around the sanctuary, will further emphasize the sense of a ``building within a building'' desired by the architects.

JACKSONVILLE JEWISH CENTER

In order to avoid the problems of surrounding urban growth at its previous facilities, the congregation of the Jacksonville Jewish Center has moved to new quarters on a semi-rural site of 37 wooded acres, which previously housed the Center's day camp. And to assure protection from future commercial encroachment, architects Freedman/Clements/Rumpel have not only located the new building at the center of its site, but have turned the building inward to relate to the central sanctuary, which is surrounded by a skylit street.

Because the Center provides a full range of community services such as schooling and social gatherings, flexibility in the required spaces to house the secular functions provided the architects with a convenient means of coping with a problem that affects all religious facilities: the seasonal changes in the number of worshippers to be accommodated in the sanctuary. (In the case of the Jewish Center, the variation in the size of the congregation ranges from approximately 400 persons to 2,000 during the High Holy Days.) Accordingly, the architects have enclosed the sanctuary with movable partitions— including that on the curvilinear track seen in the near photo at the bottom of the opposite page. This flexibility allows seating to be expanded into the social and multi-purpose rooms as needed.

Besides the essential view of the bema from the "borrowed" spaces, views of the high roof over the sanctuary (supported by steel tension-rod trusses) are seen through glazed panels, and these views further a sense of inclusion in the focal activity. The steel structure is faced with stucco on metal lath and studs.

JACKSONVILLE JEWISH CENTER, Jacksonville, Florida. Architects: *Freedman/Clements/Rumpel—Architects/Planners/Inc.—partner-in-charge: Norman Freedman; project designer: Peter Rumpel; project architect: Harleston Parkes.* Engineers: *Morales and Shumer Engineers (structural/foundation/soils); Wilder Associates (mechanical/electrical).* Acoustical consultant: *Bertram Kinzey.* General contractor: *Daniel Construction Company.*

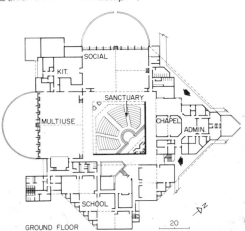

SOCIAL
KIT.
SANCTUARY
MULTIUSE
CHAPEL
ADMIN.
SCHOOL
GROUND FLOOR
20

Bob Braun photos

CHAPTER TWO:
SERVING THE SPECIFIC NEEDS
OF A RELIGIOUS COMMUNITY

Here we have monastery, mission, rectory, and religious headquarters. These buildings, set aside for special religious communities, demonstrate how spaces can be clearly differentiated for the specific use of the communities to which they belong. Several of the buildings provide living space for their users, and the separate, defined spaces stem from the special nature of the residents. Unlike those buildings designed for flexible use discussed in Chapter One, where space and even furniture are interchangeable and mobile, these buildings, designed for the specific functions of special communities, are given clearly defined and separate spaces.

Paul Rudolph, in explaining the design of the Christian Science Organization Building, says: "Flexibility is the enemy of architecture and should be limited as much as possible since it tends to become characterless." The avoidance of this quality of characterlessness echoes the concern voiced in the first chapter and affirms that the religious building must bear the stamp of, if not the architect, the community for whom it is built. While Rudolph designed the Christian Science Organization Building the way he did by choice, most of the buildings in this chapter have specific and clearly separate spaces because the many functions of religious life (worship, meditation, ritual, ceremony, celebration) are isolated from those of secular life (eating, talking, community interaction).

Monasteries illustrate this best. Take, for example, St. Vincent's. There are two kinds of activities apparent within that structure: 1) those devoted to privacy and meditation; 2) those shared by the community. Katselas carefully delineated spaces for each of these activities so that there would be no overlapping, and the harmony of the religious order is left intact. Similarly, in the rectory of Old St. Mary's, the chapel is reserved for prayer while the dining room is used for community life.

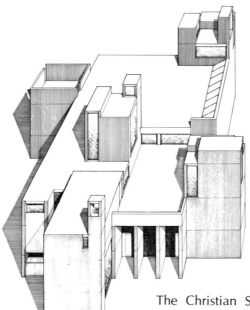

Christian Science
Organization Building

The Christian Science Organization Building in Urbana, Illinois, smaller and simpler than many of his projects, clearly shows Rudolph's alternatives to the kinds of architecture he is against. It exhibits strongly differentiated spaces which express and accent their separate and permanent functions.

Rudolph asserts that he will not create a universal space, adaptable to many uses—"flexibility is the enemy of architecture and should be limited as much as possible since it tends to become characterless." He is against what he calls "supercraftsmanship"—part of a "machine esthetic . . . in which buildings are boxes where all signs of human activity are hidden behind endlessly repeated glass or lightweight panels of absolute regularity." He is opposed to smooth machine-made finishes in buildings—to him these "seem inhuman, partially because they do not wear and consequently change with human use."

Although Rudolph's completed buildings show no signs of supercraftsmanship or the machine esthetic, his drawings suggest an architecture of great delicacy and precision. The isometric (above) and section (over-leaf) delineate a structure as meticulously finished as the drawings themselves. On the other hand, all the photographs, and the pictures on the following pages reveal that the completed building differs greatly from its pen and ink images. Although the shapes have been faithfully translated into three dimensions, the claw hammered concrete of which they are formed is rough, irregular and raw. Rudolph's drawings, sharp as steel engravings, suggest that he didn't want his *beton* to be quite so *brut* as this.

The photograph above shows the foyer and the reception area beyond. A display table in the reception area is centered within a vertical shaft into the top of which are set large glass panels of varying shapes to control the angles and intensities of light reflection. The bronze panel on the rear wall is a portrait in high relief of the founder of Christian Science, Mary Baker Eddy. Above the foyer is a T-shaped mezzanine corridor which gives access to the spaces at the second level and to the stair leading to toilet facilities and the custodian's apartment. The panels along its edge conceal lights. The room in the photograph at the left is a study space on the main floor. The desks and lighting fixtures were designed by Rudolph. The meeting hall shown on page 31 receives natural illumination from a skylight along the eastern wall, and from a tower to the north of the room. Each tower ceiling is painted in a different strong color which causes a softer hue to be reflected on the concrete walls.

The plan is designed for a corner lot. Only the eastern facade (photo), with its entrance and stair tower, and the southern facade are visible from a distance. The point at which they meet has been strongly accentuated as the focus of the design. The building, adjacent to a busy intersection on the campus of the University of Illinois, is designed to attract visits from passing students and to provide quiet spaces for meetings and religious study. This activity is concealed from the streets by continuous expanses of concrete wall. At the focal point, large areas of glass reveal the spaces within.

Rudolph has minimized the fact that the structure is quite small in contrast to an immense armory next door. Scale-giving elements such as doors and steps are recessed and unit materials such as brick or concrete block are not used. The interior is made to appear bigger than the exterior by the skillful manipulation of vertical space. Room sizes are altered by means of sliding partitions.

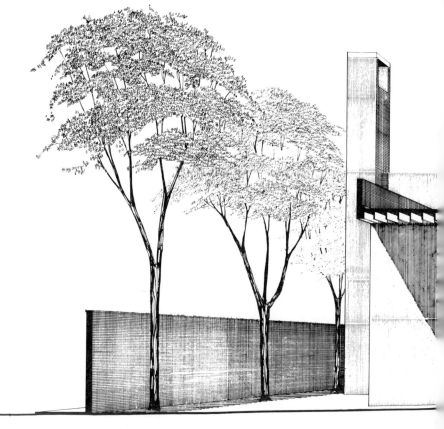

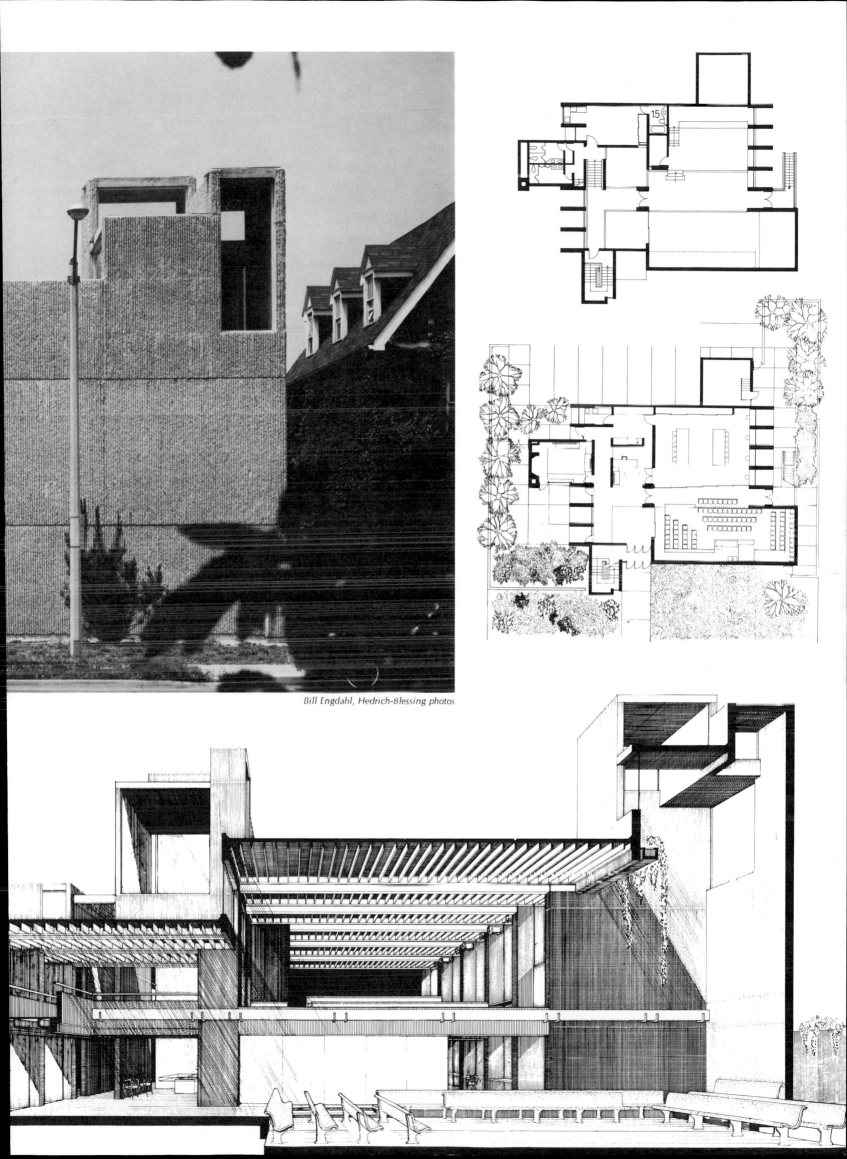

Bill Engdahl, Hedrich-Blessing photos

Vertical shaft over reception area

Lounge

Meeting Hall

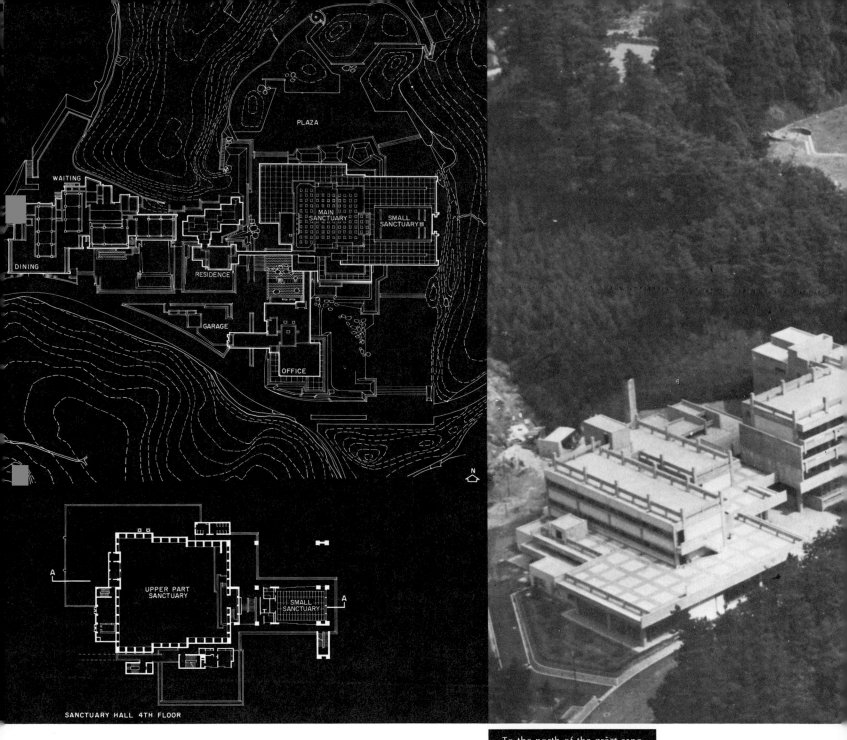

PLAZA

WAITING

DINING

RESIDENCE

MAIN SANCTUARY

SMALL SANCTUARY

GARAGE

OFFICE

N

UPPER PART SANCTUARY

SMALL SANCTUARY

A A

SANCTUARY HALL 4TH FLOOR

Tensho Kotai Jingu Sect Headquarters

BY TANEO OKI AND SACHIO OTANI

This religious sect, founded shortly after World War II and based on Shintoism, required a structure designed to accommodate their ceremonial practices. As the overall plan indicates, the plan of this religious complex in the Tabuse District of Japan's Yamaguchi Prefecture is divided into four parts and includes the founder's residence—an important symbolic structure as he is the spiritual head of this 300,000 member sect; living quarters separated by age, sex, and standing within the order; the administration building; and the sanctuaries proper. Placed on a broad plateau carved out of the hillside, the elements containing the large and small sanctuaries dominate the composition at the eastern end of the east-west axis of the complex. The elements which project southward contain the administration functions. Closer to the main axis but also projecting southward is the founder's residence. Following the downhill slope toward the west are the women's pavilion, the men's pavilion and the foreigners' pavilion which open onto broad terraces.

To the north of the great sanctuary is a large plaza. Below the smaller sanctuary is a vast sheltered open space as indicated in the section. Roofs of the lower elements serve as broad terraces and both interior and exterior spaces are linked by broad staircases. The entire complex has great plastic interest, and Otani has here achieved one of his principal design goals—the successful shaping of negative as well as positive space.

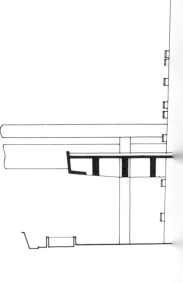

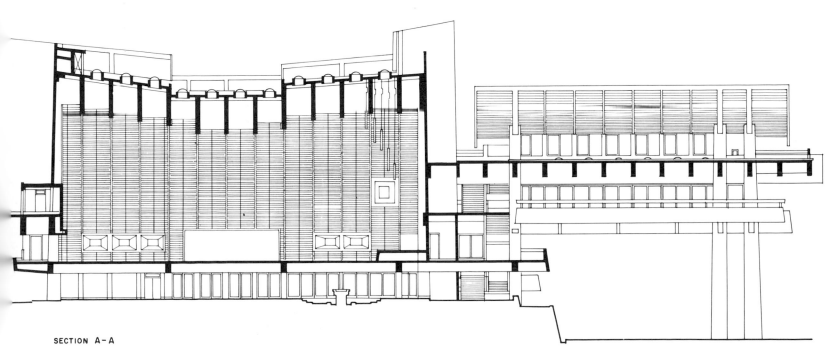

SECTION A-A

Entrance to main sanctuary

Main sanctuary

Small sanctuary

Chaminade Chapel

In an exceptionally simple and direct way, this chapel for the Marianist Missionaries' Chaminade School in south central Africa reflects and responds to the needs—climatic as well as liturgical—of a rural community in a hot and humid country. That it so successfully meets the needs of this remote location is the more remarkable for its having been designed in Cleveland, Ohio. The square plan was chosen for the straightforward, economical way the space it produces can be built. The decision to base the building on a square proved out functionally (and in line with Vatican II) as well as in construction. The altar is in the center with five rows of pews around it seating 400 people. Confessional and baptistery are in the narthex; the sacristy is on the opposite side. The site is in a clearing in the bush on which the existing school buildings are located. Since all materials had to be brought by boat to the site and all construction was by native labor, structure and materials were kept as uncomplicated as possible. Columns are of concrete block, made on the site, and trusses are of timber (safe from termites at that height). The roof is of corrugated-metal and walls are of the same material, each panel independent of its neighbor and angled differently to provide openings for ventilation along the perimeter of the building. Free circulation of air is important to comfort in that part of the world, and the ingenious handling of the wall panels allows a continuous flow of air. The overhanging roof and the angled wall panels also take care of excessive water in the rainy season.

CHAMINADE CHAPEL, Karonga, Malawi, Architects: *Richard Fleischman Architects Inc.* Engineers: *Richard Gensert Association (structural).*

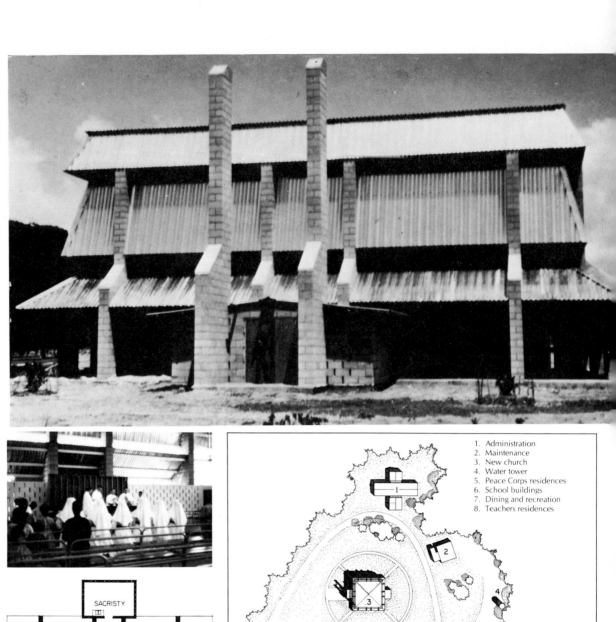

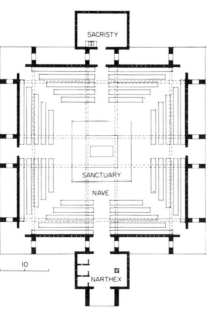

SACRISTY

SANCTUARY

NAVE

10

NARTHEX

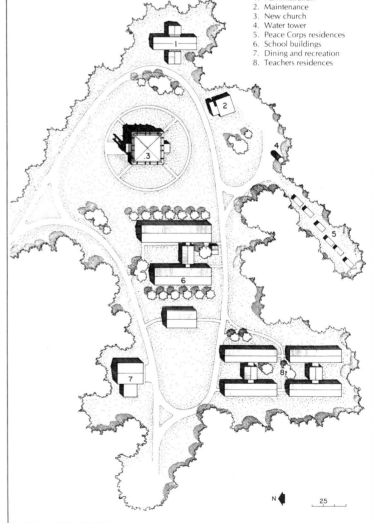

1. Administration
2. Maintenance
3. New church
4. Water tower
5. Peace Corps residences
6. School buildings
7. Dining and recreation
8. Teachers residences

N   25

Assembly Church of God Mission

This extraordinary handsome small mission church in Santo Domingo, Dominican Republic was founded by the Houston-based Assembly Church of God. The structure was designed by Austrian architect Ernst Bliem while he was a visiting professor at the University of Houston's architectural school. Morning and evening services are held each day in the small sanctuary and, during the day, the space serves as a lecture hall for the mission's students who are preparing for the ministry.

The structure is 8-in. concrete block, stuccoed and whitewashed. Concrete beams, cast on top of the walls, carry a roof structure of wood trusses, painted white which, in turn, support a roof deck of asbestos cement sheets. The floor is a slab dressed with terazzo which has been turned up, in a nice detail, to create a curb at the meeting with the wall. Screens built integrally with the walls in some sections provide natural ventilation and diffuse sunlight in a way that creates an aura of luminescence.

The mission is set on its site to create two outdoor spaces: a formal entry court with baptismal pool at the front and an active play space at the rear. The sculpture, photo below, is by the architect. Though some assistance was provided by the R.W. Johnson Construction Company and by Apex Engineering, Inc., both of Houston, most of the construction was carried out and supervised by local carpenters and masons.

The Assembly Church of God Mission is a beautifully designed structure, responsive to its tropical setting, modest and economical.

Craig Kuhner photos

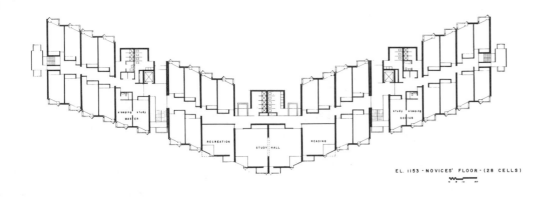

EL. 1153 · NOVICES' FLOOR · (28 CELLS)

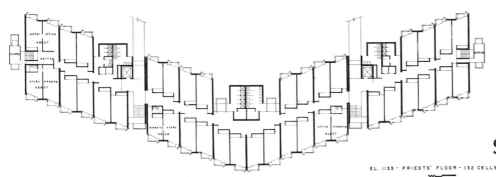

EL. 1133 · PRIESTS' FLOOR · (32 CELLS)

Plans show the arrangement of spaces at the terrace level and a typical floor. The Seminary and College is located in rolling farm land. Older monastery living quarters adjacent to the new structure were later torn down. A renovation of St. Vincent's older buildings can be seen on page 68.

St. Vincent Monastery

The Monks of St. Vincent, members of the Benedictine Order which engages in missionary activities, pastoral ministry and education, completed a new monastery on the grounds of their 121-year-old campus at Latrobe, Pennsylvania in 1967. Their architect, Tasso Katselas, had the advantage of working with a deeply committed and articulate client whose demands were subtle yet clear, and he has rewarded them with one of his finest buildings. In the words of Father Roman J. Verostko, artist and member of the College and Seminary faculty, the monks sought "a living environment which would serve them well in their search for values in their specific way of life. Each monk is provided with a private room. Architecturally designed with respect for the need of individual privacy, it provides only an indirect window-view out, creating a strong sense of being within. The architecture here serves the human need for rest, quiet, study and presence to self. On the other hand, dialogue with others and openness is encouraged with the provision of wide views toward nature to be shared in common areas such as the recreation rooms, the terraced court walks, and the roof garden. Thus the architect has created an environment which articulates the two basic demands of any community life: respect for the individual as a private and responsible person; and respect for the individual's need to share experiences."

Deglau Portraits photo; opposite page: Marc Neuhof

R oof (at top) is designed for walking. Skylights illuminate studios and novice spaces. The handsome sculptured forms shown at the right enclose the chapels, located at opposite ends of the monastery corridors. The curved exterior wall and the interior of a chapel for the infirm are shown below.

SAINT VINCENT MONASTERY, Latrobe, Pennsylvania. Owner: *Benedictine Society of Westmoreland County.* Architect: *Tasso Katselas;* structural engineers: *Richard Gensert Associates;* mechanical engineers: *Evans and Associates;* electrical engineers: *Anton J. Eichmuller and Associates;* general contractor: *Pevarnik Brothers, Inc.*

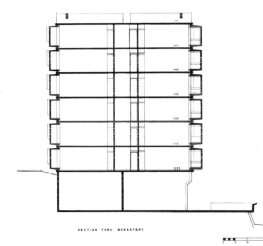

SECTION THRU MONASTERY

The portion of the cells that are supported by and cantilever beyond the V-shaped edge beams are precast. An interior space created by the alternately flat and projecting units is shown below. The relief sculpture, cast in cement, is one of several different designs by Father Verostko which are imbedded in the walls of the monastery. Each of these has been created to express a biblical word or phrase which reminds those who live there to "love one another," and to say "yes to life."

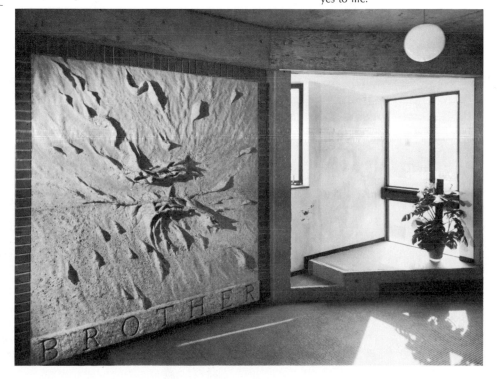

Monastery at Belmont Abbey

Rick L. Alexander, photos

This newly renovated monastery in North Carolina began life as a 33-foot-wide building with a single-loaded corridor that was designed and built by the monks of the monastery in 1881. Successive efforts added and added to it until, by 1900, it had attained the considerable length of 300 feet—still in the form of a row of rooms on three floors. The building is an unsophisticated one, containing no very important architectural feature except the most important one of all—the imprint of the people who carefully put it together. It has now been renovated with perhaps equal care to make 36 rooms for the monks, each with sinks, closets, and individual heating and air-conditioning controls. In addition, there is a six-room infir-mary with a kitchen, plus six bathrooms and a dining room, a living room, and a television room. New stairs were added to replace old ones that did not meet the code, and all walls that were not load bearing were replaced to form the new rooms. The greatest change of all was the replacement of the old windows—not, perhaps, the most desirable event, but necessary, and necessarily "modern" for what turned out to be inexorable reasons of cost.

MONASTERY AT BELMONT ABBEY, Belmont, North Carolina. Architects: *McMurray Architects + Planners.* Engineers: *King-Hudson and Associates (structural); Mechanical Engineers, Inc. (mechanical); Stephen T. Hocsek Associates (electrical).* General contractor: *Turner Construction Company.*

Old St. Mary's Parish Rectory

Replacing a 57-year old building which had been found to be unrepairable, the new Rectory was designed after Hartford Plaza was completed. It ties in with Old St. Mary's, of which it is a part, but is in no way incongruous with the Hartford building which it also closely adjoins. The obvious difference in scale is handled so appropriately that each building meets its obligations—architectural and functional—individually and naturally. The Rectory would be a handsome town house in any location; its location here is particularly happy for its effect on the city. The building's concrete frame is faced with red brick and trimmed with sand-blasted concrete, clearly recalling the old church. The entrance detail, however, is the key to the building's character: sensitively detailed, but essentially a strong and masculine building. The photograph above shows the Rectory in its setting between old and new.

OLD ST. MARY'S PARISH RECTORY, San Francisco, California. Owner: *The Roman Catholic Archbishop of San Francisco*. Architect-engineers: *Skidmore, Owings & Merrill*; general contractor: *Cahill Construction Co.*

The chapel, used daily for meditation, and for mass by visiting priests, is on the second floor, secluded yet accessible—a retreat, not from life, but to quiet. The all-white room is accented by the colors of Mark Adams' vibrant concrete-and-glass window and his softer-hued wall panel of the Stations. The dark stone altar is free-standing, with a small crucifix at its front, and the ciborium recessed in the wall behind. The chairs are from the old rectory. The dining room, also on the second floor, has both a cheerful and a monastic air. Dark-stained oak is used for trim and for the north wall with its handsomely detailed double doors and storage space crafted with old-fashioned skill. The chandelier was designed by the architects.

CHAPTER THREE:

INTERIOR DESIGN FOCUSES ON LITURGY

In all the following buildings, the design approaches show a great sense of creativity in responding to the imperatives of liturgy. We get a look at not only the over-all design of the buildings, but also the single or many facets within that make them function more efficiently for four denominations and their worship services. Acoustics, lighting, seating arrangements—all single elements—add up to the desired design of the congregation while enhancing the visual appearance of the interior. In highlighting the specific religious images of each faith, however, there is a minimum of ornamentation; instead (except for perhaps the Anshei-Sphard/Beth El Emeth Synagogue), these designs rely on simplicity and directness to focus attention on the center of worship.

In the case of the Catholic churches, the central focus being the altar, the architects keep in mind the revised liturgy according to the dictates of Vatican II, and give special attention to the participation of the people in the service. A freestanding altar, surrounded by pews in a circular pattern, allows the participants of the Mass to have a clear view and feel more a part of what is going on. Both lighting and seating, in imitating theatrical design, make the service more immediate.

Since both the altar *and* the pulpit have important places in the Protestant liturgy, Alden Dow concentrates on acoustics in the First Presbyterian Church to allow the sound of the sermon and choir to reach the congregation most effectively. Less dramatic, but no less effective, is the St. Bride's interior, recalling the beauty of Notre Dame du Ronchamp. Lighting again comes in as a vital design tool as it reflects the importance of the sanctuary.

While similar techniques are used, a more striking contrast couldn't be found than between the two temples and their interior design. Respecting the tradition of the bema as the central element of worship, the architects spotlight the sanctuary where the bema is contained and other religious symbols to create a stunning visual effect. Carefully answering the needs of a large Reform congregation and a smaller Orthodox one, the interiors may seem a bit somber in one, a bit flashy in the other, but in both, the design features are custom made for the specific philosophies of the congregations.

First Presbyterian Church

The design module for this Presbyterian church in Dearborn is a 4-foot equilateral triangle which is, in turn, the module of a hexagon. The blocks that jacket the structural steel columns emphasize the triangular motif; right and left forms of the blocks lock together to make an organic pattern. The pattern, which results from the structural system, is used on the columns and for the walls of the chapel (photos left).

Seating in the nave is arranged in two large groupings—each hexagonal in shape. The ceiling rises through a series of steps to a maximum height of 50 feet for the central, 12-foot-wide portion, which extends from the front to the rear of the church. Thus, the reverberation time over the pulpit and lectern is a minimum, and in the center—under the high ceiling—at a maximum. The choir is located directly over the narthex and center aisle to take advantage of the added reverberations for sound reinforcement. Stairs on either side of the sanctuary enable the processional to proceed from the central aisle up to the flanking balconies and encircle the congregation.

FIRST PRESBYTERIAN CHURCH OF DEARBORN, Dearborn, Michigan. Architects: *Alden B. Dow Associates;* structural engineer: *Robert J. Davis;* mechanical engineers: *Hyde & Bobbio;* general contractors: *A. Z. Schmina & Sons Company.*

St. Thomas Aquinas Church

In the Church of St. Thomas Aquinas, in Indianapolis, the firm of Woollen Associates has responded to the architectural requirements of the simplified Roman Catholic liturgy with a design of great simplicity itself. The cross in the photograph (page 53), for example, is the only one in the entire building. Nor will you see any devotional statues, softly flickering banks of votive candles, nor stainedglass windows. Gone is the romantic richness of architecture and decor, lovely and valid in its own day, but which properly belongs to eras now irrevocably dead. It has been replaced by a forthrightness and strength of design that has an immense power all its own, and a 'message' in the language of today. The kaleidoscopic array of changing meanings which the architects' vibrant red design inspires is also in keeping with the space itself. The stainless steel altar furnishings, designed by the firm, can be removed so that the great high space becomes a multi-purpose auditorium or theater.

To the left of the sanctuary stands the Blessed Sacrament chapel, an intimate space for private worship. The rich purple wall ties in with the red of the cross but does not compete with it. Tabernacles formerly stood on the main altar, but are now once again placed in a separate area. The tabernacle's transparent sides and simple shape are perfectly in keeping with the church's bare block walls and exposed services and roof structure. The narthex, below left, contains the baptismal font and the penitent's entrance to the confessional. Stairs lead to a basement sacristy.

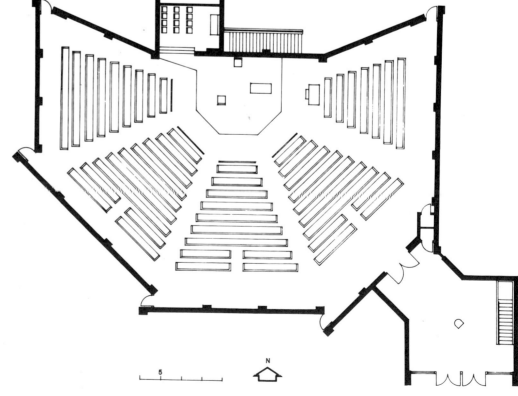

Balthazar Korab photos

The stimulus for the radically new and different kind of Catholic church architecture, of which St. Thomas Aquinas Church is an outstanding example, comes from outside the field of architecture itself. The broad aim of the Second Vatican Council was the modernization of the Church. In seeking to purify the liturgy, precepts were evolved which were aimed at giving back to the Mass more of the simplicity and spirit of the early Church. These precepts in turn were bound to drastically alter the layout and design of Catholic places of worship. The altar was made once again freestanding; the priest now faces the congregation gathered around it, all co-participants in the service, as opposed to the former long narrow nave arrangement where the average worshipper was perhaps too apt to think of himself as a spectator. In devising his own rendition of the new scheme, Woollen unabashedly borrows from modern theater design: the sanctuary becomes a thrust stage

around which the congregation is arranged on a gently sloping incline in arc-like segments. The building itself is 'bent back' to greater than 180 degrees to further the idea of the altar as the center of a great circle. Another divider between priest and participants disappears with the absence of an altar rail. Worshippers now stand, rather than kneel, to receive Communion. "A church," Woollen said at the dedication ceremonies, "is a portrait of its people at a particular moment in time." Judged in these terms St. Thomas is as resoundingly successful in fulfilling its program as anything created during that age 'when the cathedrals were white.'

ST. THOMAS AQUINAS CHURCH, Indianapolis, Indiana. Architects: *Woollen Associates—Lynn Molzan, project architect;* engineers: *Fink, Roberts and Petrie, Inc. (structural); J. M. Rotz Engineering Co., Inc. (mechanical);* liturgical consultant: *Fr. Aiden Kavanaugh, O.S.B.;* acoustical consultant: *Dr. James Hyde.*

Norman McGrath photos

Congregation Beth Torah

The sanctuary of this new synagogue for an Orthodox
community evokes a warm and sensitive religious ambience
by simple, yet powerful, architectural means. It is on a
limited site closely flanked by a tall apartment house
and two-family residences, which precluded any effective
use of side windows. Top lighting which plays on the
undulations and curves of the interior walls provides
not only an apt solution to the problem, but has been
developed into the major design feature of the space.
The skylights, fitted with artificial lights as well,
are concealed by a sculptured plaster ceiling molded
to give form and scale to the room, and by deep,
slanted wells acting as a cut-off for the lights.
In addition to those ranging the side walls, two larger
ones in the middle focus light and attention on the
centrally placed Bema and on the concave shaped Ark

wall where such significant
symbols as the Ark, Eternal
Light, and Star of David
read as isolated elements
on the white plaster surface.
Richard Foster chose an
interesting ironspot brick
for the interior and the
exterior because of its
self-cleaning quality, the
depth of coloration, and the
ease of obtaining the various
required shapes. Stone, where
used, is red sandstone and
the ornamental metal work is black anodized aluminum. The
contractor was Herbert Construction Co.; engineers were
Zoldos and Meagher (structural) and Meyer, Strong & Jones
(mechanical); consultants were Emil Antonucce (sculpture
and graphics); Ranger Farrell & Associates (acoustics) and
Richard Kelly and John L. Kilpatrick (lighting).

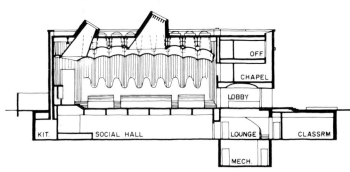

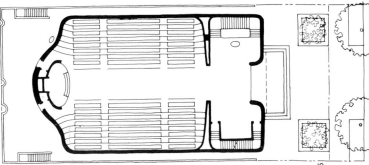

Congregations Anshei-Sphard/ Beth El Emeth

A horseshoe-shaped sanctuary that is emotive and highly charged with drama

Two Memphis congregations commissioned architects Francis Mah and Walk Jones to design a single synagogue as a center for their joint worship. Major elements in the design are a large sanctuary, a small chapel and an expansive social hall which occasionally serves both the sanctuary and the chapel as overflow space. The design for each grew out of a regularized structural system that included long bands of daylight from clerestories along transverse column lines (see plan). In the vestibule and chapel (photos, lower left), this overhead light source is a primary design tool.

The horseshoe-shaped main sanctuary is emotive and highly charged with drama. Its appeal is directly to our senses and to the emotions these senses inspire. Ranks of silver-colored, acoustical baffles hang in concentric rows from the ceiling or march in a steady cadence around the curving rear wall. Lights from sources seen and unseen pick up the colors of chair and carpet and reflect these colors from every surface. The whole interior seems suffused with color.

This arresting space, too theatrical perhaps for some, re-affirms for all how potent is interior architecture's capacity to communicate.

ANSHEI-SPHARD/BETH EL EMETH SYNAGOGUE, Memphis, Tennessee. Architects: *Mah + Jones, Inc.;* engineers: *Ellers Reaves Fanning and Oakley, Inc.* (mechanical and electrical); *Wooten-Smith & Weiss* (structural); contractor: *Grinder, Taber and Grinder, Inc.*

Otto Baitz photos

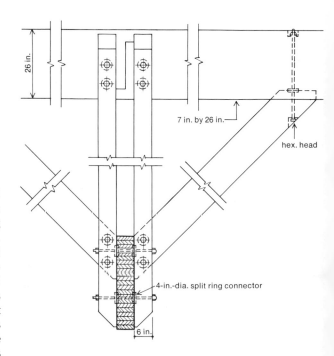

Robert E. Fischer photos

hex. head

2½ in. 5 in.

6 in. 2 in.

St. Elizabeth's Church

**In an Ohio church,
exposed roof framing,
meticulously detailed,
exalts the art of joinery**

At St. Elizabeth's Church, only the central
chapel is set aside exclusively for worship. The
adjacent hall is meant to accommodate seating
for regular services as well as other activities.
Because all furniture is movable, the exposed
roof framing provides the room's most important permanent visual element. Main structural
members are 30-in. laminated wood beams
(above) that span more than 44 ft and support
the rafters. Joints where beams, struts, rafters
and braces meet were fashioned with a fine
eye to symmetry and proportion. At the corners
of the chapel, columns were built up of four
8¼-in.-sq posts. Details at left show intersection of chapel columns and diagonal rafter
from the church hall.

CHURCH OF ST. ELIZABETH, Columbus, Ohio. Architects: *Richard Fleischman Associates.* Engineers:
Gensert Peller Mancini Associates (structural). Contractors: *C. C. Vogel Company* (general).

26 in.

7 in. by 26 in.

hex. head

4-in.-dia. split ring connector

6 in.

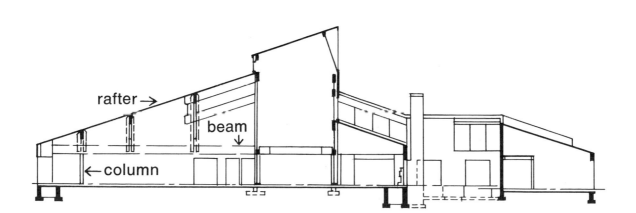

St. Bride's Church and Presbytery

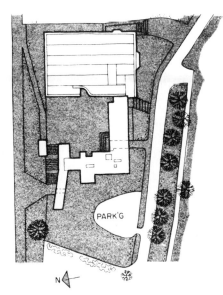

PARK'G

N

This church near Glasgow is so massive that the small buildings that form a forecourt around the entrance become almost invisible by comparison. This effect was deliberately sought by the architects, the firm of Gillespie, Kidd and Coia, so that the church would be clearly differentiated from the domestic scale of the East Kilbride neighborhood in which it is situated. Such austere monumentality captures the quality of traditional northern European brick church architecture, although the design substitutes traditional construction details for historical ornament. The interior shows that the architects are not unaware of Ronchamp, but the effect is not Corbusian. Nor does the interior resemble the rib cage of some prehistoric monster, as so many recent churches in Germany and Switzerland have done, although the church's dominating bulk, defined by structure, represents a point of resemblance to the "monster" school of ecclesiastical design.

Above: View looking towards gallery and confessionals, and view looking down into the church from the gallery. Below: the baptistry and the main entrance.

ST. BRIDE'S CHURCH AND PRESBYTERY, East Kilbride, Scotland. Architect: Gillespie, Kidd & Coia; general contractor: A. Mitchell & Sons.

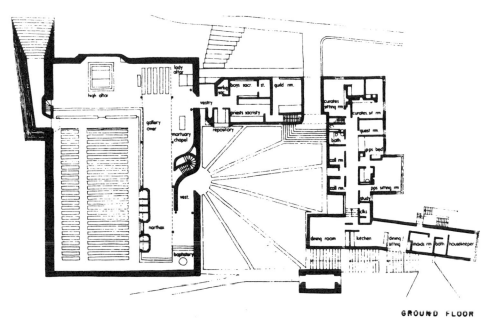

GROUND FLOOR

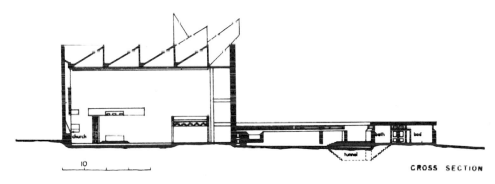

10

CROSS SECTION

The plan of the church, which seats approximately 800, is in the form of a broad rectangle, with a free-standing side gallery under which are a small chapel, confessionals and the baptistry. The entrance is a tall slot-like opening let into the west wall and curving away from the body of the church. The east wall is deeply pierced, recessed and modeled to form what the architects call "an expressive enclosing surface." The walls are of a rough-textured face brick both inside and out. The floor is of large-scale stone paving, with brick trim, and the ceiling consists of varnished pine slats concealing a steel-framed roof with standard steel glazing units. Three tall, copper-clad skylights, projecting high above the roof line throw directed lighting down on the sanctuary. Subsidiary buildings include a presbytery for the parish priest and two curates, sacristies and guild rooms. The 90-foot-high bell tower consists of two brick slabs, with slatted-timber infilling.

St. Peter Claver

The gently-sloping roof forms, the natural materials, the domestic scale and detailing are all part of a conscious effort by architects, Russell Gibson Von Dohlen to respond to the quiet residential neighborhood in West Hartford, Connecticut that surrounds the new Church of St. Peter Claver. Working with fieldstone and with cedar planking for finishes both inside and out, the architects have designed a remarkably handsome church, the heart of which is a dramatic sanctuary framed with a laminated timber roof structure connected at its joints by heavy steel plates. A series of nine skylights over the nave suffuses the center of the space with a combination of artificial and natural light (photo opposite).

In response to the design dictates established by Vatican II, the seating fans out in a quarter circle around the altar, all pews are proximate to the sanctuary, and no altar rail or other visual obstruction separates the celebrant from the congregation during services. Even stained glass, at sides and rear, is used sparingly. The simple volumetric expression and the highly restrained use of religious ornament are also signs of Vatican II reform and impart to this religious space a heightened sense of simple faith. Only a pendant bronze crucifix, with Christ's head turned upward, reminds the worshippers of the resurrection and life to come.

One result of this simplification is that St. Peter Claver's congregation has a church in which a few natural materials predominate. Floor plane, walls and ceiling structure read with elegant clarity and no design elements are visually thrown away in needless competition with other elements. All the elements receive their true—and properly propertioned—visual value.

The church contains 10,000 square feet, the nearby parish hall an additional 6,000 square feet, and a future rectory another 5,000 square feet.

ST. PETER CLAVER, West Hartford, Connecticut. Architects: *Russell Gibson Von Dohlen—John L. Riley, partner-in-charge.* Engineers: *Joseph Hallisey & Associates* (structural); *Jerome Mueller* (mechanical). Landscape architects: *Maine and Tillapugh.* Contractor: *Stanley A. Macbeth, Inc.*

Charles N. Pratt photos

The parish complex consists of a church, rectory, and multi-purpose hall. In the site plan, the church assumes the central location of primary focus and is flanked left and right by the other two structures. The rectory, to be built later, will be isolated by an access road from the other two. Though the site planning seems sensible, and the wish to preserve the natural character of the site is commendable, one wishes the parking requirements had not been so heavy or that some system of off-street parking had been practical.

CHAPTER FOUR:
RENOVATION, RESTORATION, EXPANSION

Renovation is increasingly becoming a desirable and necessary alternative to replacing rundown buildings. Rather than tear down what is merely unused or old, more people are recognizing the permanent value and economic feasibility of renovation or restoration. Renovation can serve an especially useful purpose for religious buildings, as it not only restores mechanical and material malfunctions, but also offers the opportunity to update the interior and include revised liturgical functions.

What still stands that is valid and functional? How can I incorporate the old system into the new and vice versa? These questions confront the conscientious architect as he taps every available resource in the old building to convert and adapt it into a better and lasting new one. Tasso Katselas had the good fortune to find a still-usable underground passageway which he in turn used for circulation from one building to the other on the massive St. Vincent's monastery campus. His concern with carrying over the continuity and order that existed in the original building shows in the harmony of the newly furnished structure.

Philip Ives, in his careful attention to the most minute detail in St. Jude's chapel, designed this lovely renovation in the midst of busy Georgetown. A sense of harmony is achieved through his arrangement of furniture and fixtures which create such a balanced effect that we haven't a clue as to which were in the old building and which were added for the renovation.

We have included additions and expansions in this chapter because they present problems similar to the problems of renovations. There is an original building which the architect must integrate with a new one, or must add something to. The Unitarian Center, for example, in its addition, demonstrates how sensitivity to the shape and site of the older buildings can be integrated for a harmonious expansion of space for the community involved.

St. Vincent Monastery

Boniface Wimmer was the monastery's first abbott. On the adjacent property he and his successors acquired, Katselas is now planning a new community to be called Wimmerton.

John Hobbs photos

St. Vincent Monastery outside Pittsburgh is a complex of buildings, the earliest of which was constructed about 125 years ago. The various buildings are stylistically divergent but each is fashioned of handmade brick by masons who obviously took special delight in the work of their hands.

When fire gutted many of the buildings a decade ago, Tasso Katselas was commissioned to prepare a new master plan—or "master concept" as he prefers to describe it—that envisioned a series of changes extensive in scope and duration. The newer work—extensive in itself—included a new main entrance to the administrative wing (photo left). This required removing an old warehouse and relocating the nun's quarters to a new portion of the campus-like plan. To create a new reception area, Katselas removed the floor of one space (photo right), but left in place the existing system of wood beams notched to receive floor joists. While visiting is somewhat restricted, this space has become a hub of activities and the monastery staff wonders how it got along for a century without such a space.

In the course of removing old materials and finishes, Katselas has found a variety of old spaces of unusual interest. An old milk cellar, for instance, was uncovered adjacent to the reception area shown at right and it was subsequently converted into a meditation and conference space.

Under the monastery, and connecting many of its buildings, Katselas found a labyrinthine series of interconnected tunnels, some of them for access to mechanical services, but others that included beautifully built spaces with vaulted stone ceilings. These will be retained and renovated to provide covered (albeit underground) circulation between the buildings.

While St. Vincent's represents renovation at an unusually large scale, Katselas has been careful to retain much of what was good and has resisted the temptation to replace indiscriminately those elements that give St. Vincent's and its brotherhood a sense of continuity and order.

RENOVATION OF ST. VINCENT MONASTERY, Latrobe, Pennsylvania. Architect: *Tasso Katselas.* Engineers: *R. M. Gensert and Associates* (structural); *Environment Inc.* (mechanical/electrical); Landscape consultant: *Joseph Hajains.* Contractors: *Pivarnik Brothers and Dill Construction Company.*

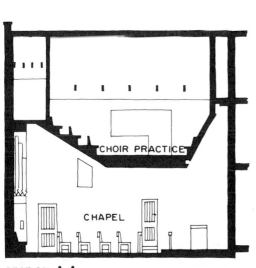

SECTION A-A

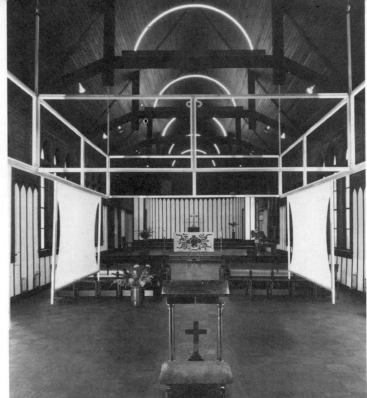

Belton S. Wall photos

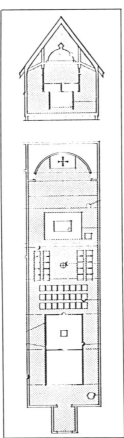

St. Mary's Episcopal Church

The renovation of this small church made good use of a building which had fallen into disrepair, and it attempted to invest it as well with an altogether new character which, it was hoped, would be appropriate to a liturgical form that had changed radically since the original church had been built. The adaptation, though, sought to respect as much as possible the character of the original structure, shifting the tone to the more contemporary mainly by application of new elements, rather than by radically altering the old ones. Thus the bulk of the renovation consisted of providing new furnishings, new lighting, and new mechanical systems—plus simply refurbishing what was already there. Flexibility is the key here: the new seating is composed of interlocking single chairs, there is no fixed pulpit, nor is there a communion rail, and the altar is completely portable. Panels of nylon stretched on aluminum frames allow spaces to be defined differently for different functions, and neon arches were added above to create the feeling of a festive atmosphere—and to induce some light up near the dark ceiling. Track lighting, in addition, is used to provide supplementary lighting when needed during the day, and primary lighting at night.

ST. MARY'S EPISCOPAL CHURCH, Jacksonville, Florida. Architects: *Freedman/Clements/Rumpel.* General contractor: *Jenkins Construction Company.*

72

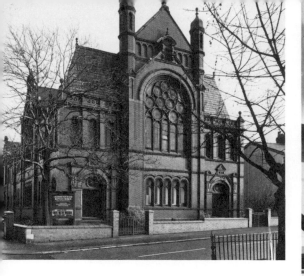

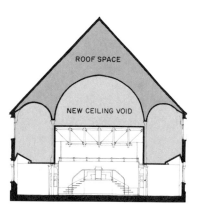

ROOF SPACE

NEW CEILING VOID

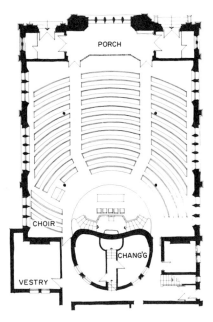

PORCH

CHOIR

CHANG'G

VESTRY

Leamington Road Baptist Church

The architects of this radical restoration were initially commissioned to design an altogether new building to replace the one which is shown above. They duly noted, however, that, in addition to a rather small budget for the required new program, they were being presented with an older building which made a considerable and memorable impression in its neighborhood. Its basic problem was that it was vast and therefore extremely expensive to heat and otherwise to maintain, and it was also beset with a particularly bad case of dry rot, which would have to be arrested immediately if the building were to survive. And so it was arrested, the shell of the existing building was retained, and a two-thirds smaller (in volume)

and more modern interior was composed inside it. Existing cast iron columns were used as a basic structure from which to hang wooden trusses at varying levels; these in turn were left exposed, and they support the lightweight timber ceiling. The windows at the ground floor level were left exposed, to give light inside, and the new strongly profiled ceiling was cocooned in fiberglass taken down the paneling of the external walls to give a very high level of thermal insulation.

LEAMINGTON ROAD BAPTIST CHURCH, Blackburn, England. Architects and engineers: *Building Design Partnership*. Partner-in-charge: *N. K. Scott;* General contractors: *Henry Ibbotson and Sons, Limited.*

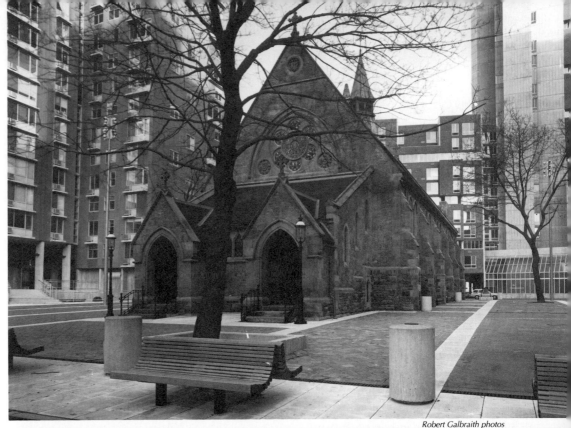

Robert Galbraith photos

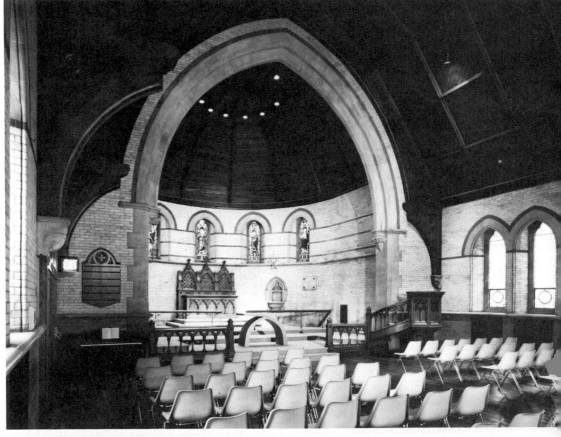

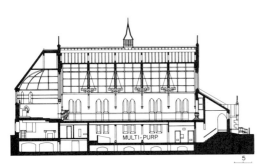

MULTI-PURP

5

Chapel of the Good Shepherd

The Chapel of the Good Shepherd on Roosevelt Island in New York was designed in 1875 by Frederick Withers, a one-time partner of Calvert Vaux, one of the architects for Central Park. It has been restored as a community building with a religious focus for the burgeoning Roosevelt Island new town. The design problem in this case involves an intriguing host of technical problems, rather than any dramatic alteration of the old building's appearance. Current code requirements, for instance, call for windows about six times the present size for ventilation (which is therefore accomplished mechanically), and a good deal of structural reinforcing (by new steel beams) was required. Access for the handicapped also had to be provided, and the front stairs had to be supplemented with an additional stairway reached from the opposite direction, which was finally placed in the bottom of the bell tower, with new mechanical equipment in the top. All of this, as well as the needs of the community, increased the urgency for the building to become a multiple-use structure in order to raise the required money for its preservation.

CHAPEL OF THE GOOD SHEPHERD, Roosevelt Island, New York, New York. Architect: *Giorgio Cavaglieri—project manager: Denis Glen Kuhn.* Architects for the plaza landscaping: *Johansen & Bhavnani.* Engineers: *Hecht, Hartmen & Concessi (mechanical).* General contractor: *Calcedo Construction Corporation.*

Philip Molten photos

Unitarian Center

Redevelopment in San Francisco's Western Addition gave the First Unitarian Church the opportunity to expand both its physical property and its program of activities within the community. The new buildings provide facilities where groups of various sizes, from 15 to 400, can meet, and these are made available for use by the community as well as by church members and organizations. There are also new church offices, a church school, an art room, a child care center, and a new chapel. The new structures are placed on the perimeter of the site, leaving a central atrium which is used, in good weather, as a social center. Daylight from the atrium floods a spacious gallery which surrounds it and which is both an exhibition area and the main circulation for the complex. The old church—built in 1889, and a survivor of the 1906 earthquake—and the new buildings achieve a remarkable harmony despite the difference in their styles and the periods they represent.

THE UNITARIAN CENTER, San Francisco, California. Architects: *Callister, Payne & Rosse.* Engineers: *Stefan Medwadowski,* structural; *O'Kelly & Schoenlank,* mechanical & electrical. Landscape architect: *John Carmack.* Contractor: *Pacific Coast Builders.*

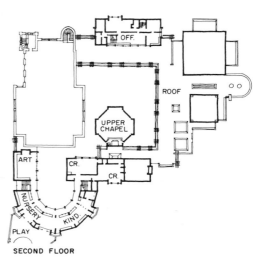

SECOND FLOOR

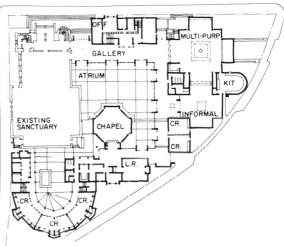

FIRST FLOOR

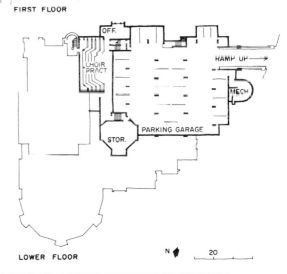

N 20

LOWER FLOOR

The handsome rough-form concrete stairs (above) lead to nursery and kindergarten. The chapel connects by the gallery (left) with the meeting rooms and is just a few yards from the old church. The multi-purpose room (below) and adjoining informal room are the main facilities for parish social activities. Under this area is a garage for 36 cars and a choir practice room which doubles as a small arena theater.

Philip Molten photos

Northwoods Presbyterian Church

When the congregation for the Northwoods Presbyterian Church in Doraville, Georgia decided to expand its facilities, architect Jack D. Haynes was retained to design the addition. The program called for a new sanctuary seating 500 worshippers, new classrooms which will double during the week as kindergarten space, and parking for 150 cars.

The original structure consisted of a square fellowship hall surrounded by classrooms and on all sides by a narrow porch. Haynes retained the existing building, converting the north porch into circulation space that serves a new semi-circular sanctuary that centers on a raised altar platform. Two floors of new classroom space have been added in a split level arrangement to the east elevation of the existing building. New educational space, should it ever become necessary, can be added in similar increments to the building's other elevations. A bell tower on the east side of the new sanctuary completes the addition.

Construction materials are simple and economically assembled—stuccoed concrete block for bearing walls, bar joists for supporting upper floors and roof. Over the sanctuary, Haynes has used a radial pattern of fir 2x8s. This ceiling, suspended from the roof structure, screens out ductwork and diffusers located above and painted flat black. It also serves as an architectural device to focus attention on the area of the altar.

What lifts the Northwoods Presbyterian addition above many similar projects is the naturalness and simplicity with which old and new structure have been sensitively joined. There is dignity and elegance here but they have not come—as they sometimes have elsewhere—at the expense of liturgical function.

NORTHWOODS PRESBYTERIAN CHURCH, Doraville, Georgia. Architect: *Jack Durham Haynes.* Engineers: *Jack K. Wilborn* (structural); *Hartrampf, Powell and Associates* (mechanical); *Edwards and Rosser* (electrical). Landscape architect: *John Patton.* Acoustical consultant: *John R. Ballentine.* Contractor: *Aderhold Construction Co.*

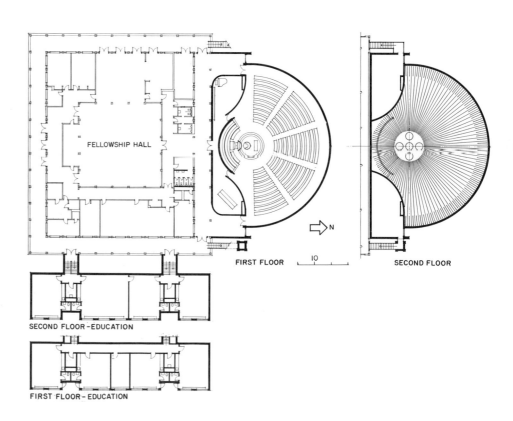

FELLOWSHIP HALL

FIRST FLOOR

N

SECOND FLOOR

SECOND FLOOR-EDUCATION

FIRST FLOOR-EDUCATION

New Ministries Building, Park Street Church

Architects Stahl/Bennett were selected for the new Ministries Building of Boston's architecturally distinguished Park Street Church of 1803 because of their previous restoration work on period buildings, and the client assumed they would produce a similar structure from "whole fabric." It took six months of dialogue to convince the building committee that a "reproduction" similar to that which the members envisioned (drawing above) would be insulting to an authentic building, unproductive to the church's causes (by producing a backward-looking image) and unworkable in practical terms. A phenomenon in current religious experience, Park Street is constantly growing in membership and (possibly causative) social and religious programs. Its space needs for Sunday School functions alone were projected to soon almost fill the 22,500 square feet of the eventual building. Other functions to be accommodated included administration, counseling, accounting, nursery, tourist orientation and social (Recognizing the space demands, the original "in-house" proposal envisioned a building actually extending over the church.)

In order to reduce the visible bulk, the architects designed a truly loft-type building that could alternately accommodate the needed various functions within the same areas (a concept consistent with those discussed on pages xii-20)—placing a fixed-function gymnasium in an excavated basement. The concept of flexible and columnless floors is expressed on the exterior by the butt-jointed glass of the windows, giving an unobstructed view from within and inviting participation from without. Typical of many additive buildings, the structure consists of varied parts: a concrete wall on the elevator side and columns that allow the long-covered original wall of the church to be exposed on the other. Air handling ducts are run only vertically (between the columns and the church's wall) to reduce floor-to-floor heights. This helps to bring the new building into a desired height alignment with the existing building on the other side of the church.

NEW MINISTRIES BUILDING, PARK STREET CHURCH, Boston, Massachusetts. Owner: *Trustees of the Park Street Church.* Architects: *Stahl/Bennett, Inc.—principal-in-charge: Frederick A. Stahl; project architect: Martin S. Lehman.* Engineers: *LeMessurier Associates, Inc.* (structural); *Golder Gass Associates, Inc.* (foundation/soils); *Shooshanian Engineering Associates* (mechanical/electrical). Consultants: *William Lam Associates* (lighting). General contractor: *Barkan Construction Co.*

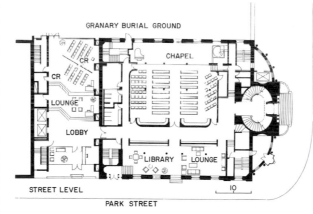

GRANARY BURIAL GROUND

CHAPEL

CR
CR
LOUNGE
LOBBY
LIBRARY LOUNGE

STREET LEVEL

PARK STREET

Steve Rosenthal photos

The client requirement of a dramatic space for social functions produced the double-height room at the top of the building facing the adjacent park (see section and photo, above). This room conceals the two-story mechanical space. Both the building and its furnishings (photo, below) are very different from that first envisioned by the client (drawing, top). Future plans call for the rehabilitation of the ground floor of the original church to accommodate expanded functions and tie the circulation of the two buildings together (plan, left). The second, third and fourth floors have movable furniture that allows the same space to serve as offices, meeting rooms, or Sunday school space.

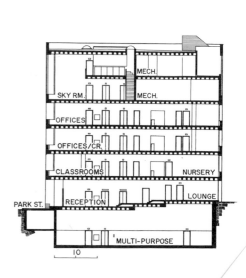

MECH.
SKY RM. MECH.
OFFICES
OFFICES/CR.
CLASSROOMS NURSERY
PARK ST. RECEPTION LOUNGE
MULTI-PURPOSE

CHAPTER FIVE:
DRAMATIC SHAPES

When seen from the exterior, all nine of these dramatically shaped buildings cut striking profiles into their various sites, and test our preconceived notions of what churches and temples ought to look like. In the structures that follow, we see what possible shapes churches can take. From following the geometry of form, from imitating natural shapes, these buildings, while appealing to our sculptural sense, express the hope and community of religious experience.

For its geometric sculpture, Tigerman's Benedictine Chapel stands out as one of the more powerful shapes. Consisting of a circular series of triangles, the church, if viewed from above, might look like a crown of thorns. Although this spiny exterior jolts the viewer into adjusting to a structure that seems to bristle in defense, the interior embraces those who enter, evoking an aura of intimacy and community which might be compared to the underground catacombs.

In the organic shape of the Temple Beth El, the architect took as his inspiration the marine mollusk. He articulately explains this reasoning for wanting "to create an aura of ascending space while utilizing the engulfing atmosphere of the circle. A special interior space must exist in religious buildings, a space that is functional but is in itself an inspirational element."

Whether they recall hyperbolic paraboloid, tent-like helix, or Wrightian geometry, these buildings embody religious experience, symbols, and belief through the expression of their dynamic structures. Pietro Belluschi, consultant for St. Mary's Cathedral, explains the goal of that building and perhaps of all the buildings in this chapter: "If it is to endure as a symbol of our faith and of our seriousness as builders, it must consist of elemental forms, handled with the kind of simplicity that becomes both structure and symbol, to be looked at and remembered."

Episcopal Church of the Epiphany

Walter Wagner

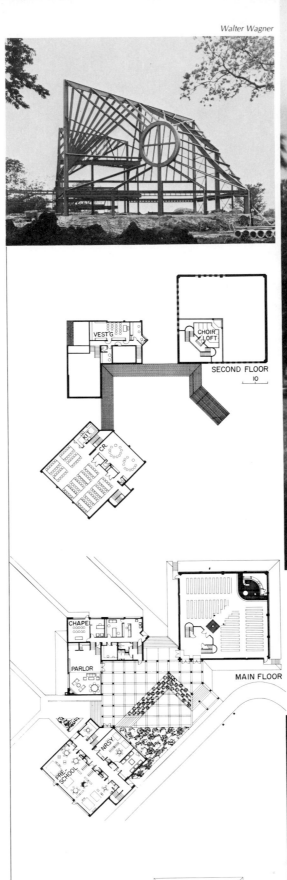

The approach to this church in suburban Houston is of course dominated by the roof form with its round stained glass window. But upon arrival, churchgoers experience a simply-managed but effective circulation amidst low and simple buildings with somewhat ceremonial changes of elevation and scale—until they emerge from beneath the choir loft into the sanctuary, where roof shape, seating arrangement, and the light from the window combine to focus attention on the chancel.

Designed to be a strong community focus, the complex is set in a triangular plan—with an administration and social building set between the sanctuary and the education building. The simplicity and scale of the secondary buildings establishes a scale of importance that is strengthened, physically and psychologically, by raising the plaza and the sanctuary five-and-a-half feet on fill—an astonishingly successful technique on the bald prairie surrounding the church.

The raised plaza also works well to relate all of the subsidiary spaces by permitting a split-level plan in the administration and education buildings. The social "parlor" is at "piazza" level, with offices and a high-ceilinged chapel a half flight down and vesting rooms above. In the education building, nursery and Sunday-school spaces are a half-flight down; the fellowship hall a half flight up. The result is a compact, multi-level space arrangement with none of the too-familiar "church basement" feeling. In a colder climate, of course, the outdoor circulation would have to be modified.

EPISCOPAL CHURCH OF THE EPIPHANY, Houston. Architects: *Clovis Heimsath Associates Inc.*—project team: *Clovis Heimsath, John Day, and Fred Stephens.* Engineers: *Krahl & Gaddy Engineers* (structural), *Jochen & Henderson, Inc.* (mechanical and electrical). Liturgical consultant: *Rambusch Associates.* Landscape: *Fred Buxton.* Contractor: *BD & B, Inc.*

Ed Stewart photos

The complex roof was framed, as the construction photo above left shows, entirely in straight members—the double curvature formed by placing the diagonal of the roof above the square of the base and running straight members between. The shape is sheathed in wood. Elsewhere materials were chosen to lend a sense of tradition—light brown brick for most exterior walls, with rough native rubble stone forming the lower walls of the sanctuary structure inside and out. Heavy timbers atop brick columns support the arcade roof. All sloping roofs are cedar shake.

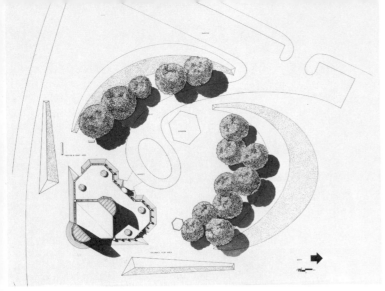

Elk Grove
United Presbyterian Church

Lionel Freedman photos

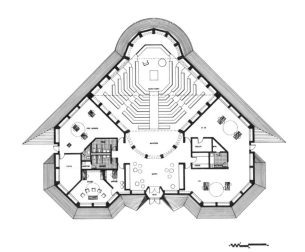

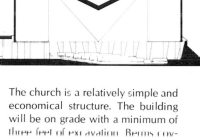

Architect Ulrich Franzen is singularly able, as in this church project, to produce an accomplished synthesis of assorted stylistic elements, each of which has been boldly stated and correctly used. This design makes no effort to conceal its debt to Frank Lloyd Wright, Le Corbusier, and their distinguished disciple Louis Kahn.

The plan, Wrightian in its geometry, neatly articulates the separation and contrast between the low-ceilinged, intimate quality of the teaching space and the vertical thrusts of the worship space. The latter is shaped by two great skylit shafts which come to Elk Grove by way of Chandigarh and Rochester. To have been built of laminated wood arches and beams, they would have been covered with aluminum on the exterior, and given an impression of lightness neatly juxtaposed against the church's heavy masonry base. The horizontal element would have its own skylights, similar to forms which first gained widespread attention when they appeared as light sources for the chapels at Corbu's Monastery of La Tourette.

The church would rest upon an open flat plain and be surrounded by built-for-sale houses typical of mobile young middle-class families. Franzen strove to achieve a sense of *place* for this house of worship, by working with elements which suggest permanence and enclosure.

The solid appearing textured concrete block walls and the carefully sculptured berms shown in the plot plan and model photograph at left, are designed in a manner to reconcile opposites. These forms help distinguish the church from its surroundings, and establish its separateness and importance — yet at the same time they reach out, invite and welcome the worshipper into the religious precinct, and then contain him within it.

The church, as of publication date, has not been built.

The church is a relatively simple and economical structure. The building will be on grade with a minimum of three feet of excavation. Berms covered with flat cast-concrete pavers extend to the clerestory windows of the classroom element.

ELK GROVE UNITED PRESBYTERIAN CHURCH, Elk Grove Village, Illinois — pastor: Reverend Robert G. Long. Architects: *Ulrich Franzen and Associates — associate-in-charge, Samuel E. Nylen;* structural engineers: *Garfinkel Marenberg and Associates.* mechanical engineer. *J. L. Altieri.*

St. Benedict's Abbey Church

St. Benedict's Abbey Church is on rolling land which overlooks Benet Lake. The main sanctuary seats 300 laymen with choir stalls for a maximum of 36 monks. The altar is at the far end, although the plan would also function well if the altar were at the center. The church serves as a principal entry to the monastery proper. Access to and from the monastery is by means of a double ramp and connecting corridor which passes through the exposed concrete wedge-shaped link, passing under the hollow cylinder in which the bell is hung.

The plan provides for two different kinds of ceremonial processions, and its two major axes form a cross which is expressed in the roof truss system as well as the plan.

No actual Cross appears on the church exterior, but one of rusted metal, made by a member of the Order can be seen in the photo on page 91. Tigerman intended his building to resemble a church only in the sense that it functions as a church. By avoiding a linear hierarchic plan with an overwhelmingly dominant axis he created a more intimate space that tends to surround and embrace the congregation. The plan shape encourages active community and lay participation in the service.

The church is basically a 68-foot square concrete box concealed by an 8-foot-wide sloping earth berm. The geometrically ingenious roof is not as complex as it appears at first glance. It consists of ten simple trusses of laminated beechwood. Tigerman has created his sloping planes by leaving out the top horizontal chords of the perimeter trusses as the diagram below indicates. The vertical planes on the perimeter are surfaced in metal. The others are glazed with solar bronze glass forming clerestories which dramatically light the main sanctuary. The interior of the church is as simple and direct in its juxtaposition of functional elements and its use and forming of materials as is the exterior. The connecting bridge from the monastery appears in the three photos at left. Like the double ramp to which it connects, it is emphatically separated from the adjacent exposed concrete walls. These walls thus appear as continuous surfaces which adjoin the remaining walls of the sanctuary to form one unbroken concrete envelope. The ceiling is sharply defined from the walls by the straightforward use of beechwood trusses and interior decking, as well as by the solar glass. Even the carpet has its own clearly articulated edge.

ST. BENEDICT'S ABBEY CHURCH, Benet Lake, Wisconsin. Owner: *The Benedictine Fathers*. Architects: *Stanley Tigerman of Stanley Tigerman & Associates—associates: John F. Fleming and Anthony Saifuku*; engineers: *The Engineers Collaborative* (structural); *Walter Flood & Company* (foundation and soils); *Wallace & Migdal* (mechanical and electrical); general contractor: *Pepper Construction Company*.

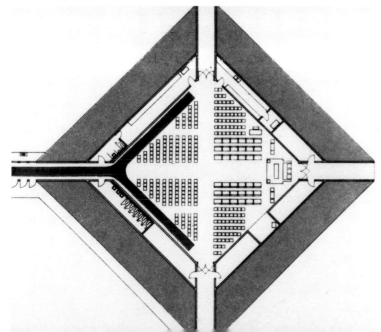

The exterior of St. Benedict's Abbey Church in Benet Lake, Wisconsin refocuses the eye and challenges one's preconceptions about how a church should look. In essence the structure appears to be a roof and a base with no building in between—rather like one of sculptor-painter René Magritte's somber images of hats perched on shoulders instead of heads. There is something curiously dissatisfying in the lack of transition between the terne-coated stainless steel roof and the sodded grass berms which surround the chapel. The only unity between roof and berms is a common geometry of triangular and trapezoidal planes. The building appears scaleless, due in part to the fact that the doors are hidden in deep reveals and other elements which clarify scale are invisible or absent. Acquaintance with architect Tigerman's sculptures (below) might cause one to suspect that their creator has too eagerly and inappropriately seized the opportunity to inflate one of his tetrahedral constructs to church size

Such first thoughts are soon followed, however, by the realization that Tigerman was purposefully attempting to create exterior forms of indefinite scale which are at the same time modest and unpretentious. The triangular-shaped vertical walls and sloping roof planes were carefully sized to diminish the scale of the four-story tudor-style monastery structure to which the chapel is attached. It becomes clear also that Tigerman deliberately strove for a spare economical look which would not at the same time appear mean and stingy. What could be more eloquently and generously simple than a building for worship sheathed in metal, glass and grass?

The principal structural materials are exposed and no veneers or facings have been used. Since the bulk of the building has been constructed below ground, heat loss or gain is minimized and energy thus conserved. Prototypes for the triangulated St. Benedict's Abbey Church are easy to find in architect Tigerman's work as a painted and sculptor, as well as in some of his earlier visionary projects. His "Urban Matrix" (far right) proposes inverse pyramids for habitation on water. Shown below is "Instant City," a grouping of self-contained housing and office pyramids which would span expressways. St. Benedict's would seem to be most truly pre-figured however by "Modsculp II" (middle) which is made up of cube-octahedrons which can be arranged in a number of configurations.

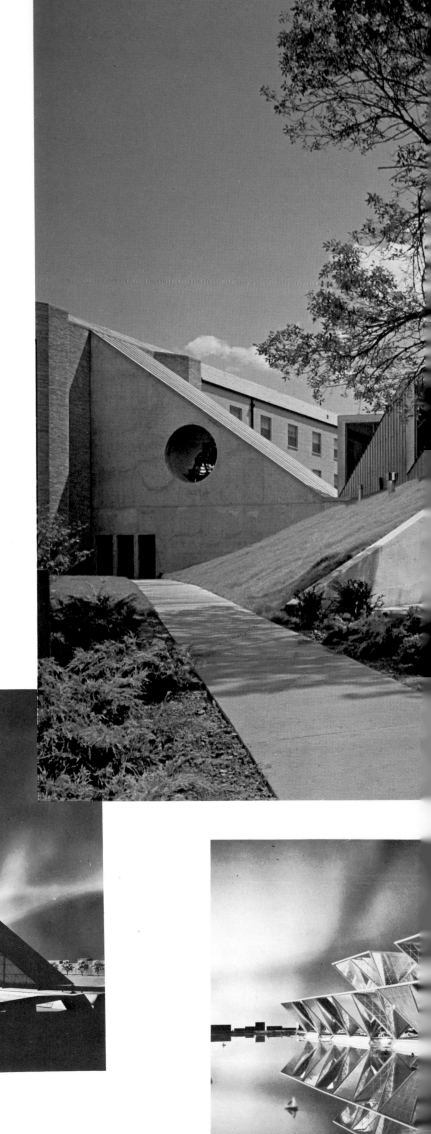

all photos © Morley Baer except where noted

St. Mary's Cathedral

Designing a cathedral is the most coveted—and rarest—of architectural experiences. In the past decade only a handful of cathedrals have been built in the world. Of these the first to base its concept in the new liturgy of the Catholic church is St. Mary's, San Francisco, a cathedral as surely of its time as the great medieval cathedrals were of theirs.

The new cathedral of San Francisco takes the place of the red brick Victorian Gothic building, built in 1887, which burned to the ground in September 1962. Hardly had the ashes of the old cathedral cooled when speculation began as to who would design the new: surely only a world-famous architect would be chosen for so prestigious a job in such a city as San

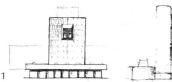

1   2

Francisco. Announcement made in the following April that the little-known firms of Angus McSweeney and Ryan and Lee had been appointed, caught the whole community unawares. There was first amazement, then consternation, then strong —and vocal—pressure (especially from wealthy and influential donors) for a change of architects. The archdiocese maintained its commitment to the local firms, but it did acquiesce to their suggestion that an architect of world renown be appointed to work with them on the design.

The man on whom all agreed was Pietro Belluschi of Boston, Italian by birth, engineer by training, architect by choice and long experience, Catholic by upbringing, and the designer of some of this country's most distin-

3

guished churches. At first Belluschi did not want the job; he knew what agony of spirit such a job would entail, and how long it would take. Besides, in his innate modesty, he felt that he could not do it justice. "My talents had been nourished on less ambitious proj-

ects," he says. "But like the reluctant bride, in the end I could not resist the seduction."

His modesty and his reluctance were unjustified. No more fortunate choice could have been made. Belluschi's extensive experience as consultant on projects of great variety and scope, his work with a diversity of minds and temperaments, and the restraint and elegance of his taste, were exactly the ingredients needed. His appointment was announced in September, although he had been working through the summer with the

5   6

local architects and he had already formed the concept which later became the design of the new cathedral. Because of the engineering inherent in the concept, he had asked that Pier Luigi Nervi be retained as consultant

Morley Baer   ELLIS STREET

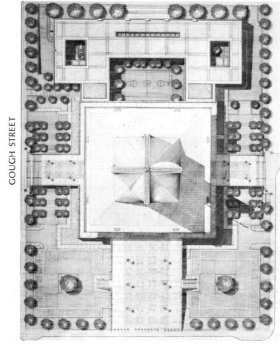

GOUGH STREET   OCTAVIA STREET

GEARY STREET

Morley Baer

Morley Baer

"The essence of contemporary architecture is not the avoidance of style, or the creating of a new one, but an insistence on integrity of thought," wrote Pietro Belluschi to the Archbishop. Integrity, proportion and clarity—Thomas Aquinas' guiding principles for greatness—are the essence of the design so majestically achieved in St. Mary's. The cathedral stands free on the crest of Cathedral Hill, the highest eminence in that part of the city, the Western Addition redevelopment area. The principal entrance is on the north instead of the west (as in most European cathedrals.) It is approached from Geary Street, on the high side of the site, across a great plaza or forecourt, 200 feet wide and 150 feet deep. From this plaza the scale of the building and the full sweep of the 190-foot-height of the cupola can be seen. The entire structure is covered with travertine marble, the utter simplicity of its use a subtle foil for the richness of the material. Stairs

from the plaza lead to the parking area and to the entrance to the 1,200-seat cathedral hall and other meeting rooms, sacristy and kitchen. The rectory, a convent and a high school are on the south side of the site.

"What would Michelangelo have thought of this cathedral?" the designers were asked at the unveiling of the final design. Nervi answered for all: "He could not have thought of it. This design comes from geometric theories not then proven. It could only have been conceived today."

on engineering design, and Nervi's appointment was announced simultaneously with Belluschi's.

The early Belluschi design proposals (1, 2, 3, 4) show a more or less traditional approach, following the direction taken by McSweeney, Ryan and Lee who were striving to meet both

7

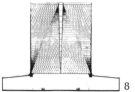

8

the program and the wishes of Archbishop Joseph T. McGucken and Monsignor Thomas J. Bowe, pastor of St. Mary's, whose first inclination had been toward a design developed from the historic Mission Dolores in San Francisco. But Belluschi's search for form did not stop with the conventional even though any one of his early approaches would have made a beautiful building. His conviction was

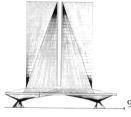

strong that the design of a cathedral for today, if it was to "endure as a symbol of our faith and of our seriousness as builders" must consist of elemental forms, handled with the "kind of simplicity that becomes both structure and symbol, to be looked at and remembered." The more he struggled with the problem, the more certain he became that "here was a need for a strong structural concept—an engineering form as an expression of the modern age, comparable in scale and size to the cathedrals of the past, a form that could only be done now. And I knew that it was nec-

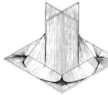

10

essary to have someone like Nervi to help in its fulfillment.

"The idea of using a warped surface for the envelope of the cathedral came to me from the studies and drawings of the Catalanos, close friends and associates at M.I.T., which had been published in 1960 in the student publication of the North Carolina School of Design. My first tentative sketches (5, 6) were made in September 1963. In hundreds of other sketches I explored

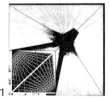

11

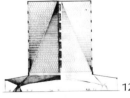

12

all aspects of the design, but these have the essence of the idea."

Coincident with this breakthrough in design was the announcement by the Second Vatican Council of a new constitution of sacred liturgy. The new design concept had, fortuitously, pre-

Gyorgy Kepes

The interior of St. Mary's is neither dim nor mysterious; there are no unseeable recesses, no barriers, gates or grills. Yet there is drama nevertheless, expressed in the structure itself; the plain surfaces and the clear lines of the arches contrast with the rich coffers of the cupola, Kepes' glowing colors on its curving surfaces, and Lippold's baldacchino a glistening announcement of the cathedral's focal point.

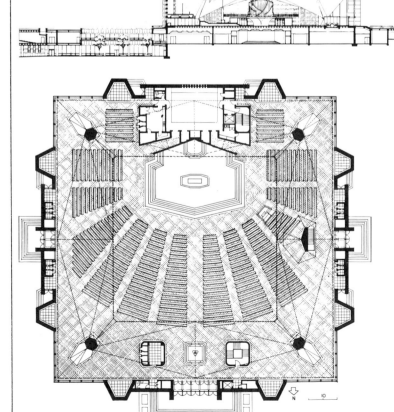

figured the architectural implications of the Council's directive that priest and people should be united with the altar as their focus. Under the great cupola of Belluschi's scheme, in a single unobstructed space, were sanctuary, nave, baptistery and narthex.

Although Nervi had had no previous direct experience with hyperbolic paraboloids, he set to work immediately and enthusiastically to find the structural solution (7, 8, preliminary; 11, 12 final) for the concept. In his usual way, he had models made and tested at the Instituto Sperimentale Modelli Structure in Bergamo. The first results were discouraging, but a modified design and new, larger models brought ultimate success. Belluschi continued to study structure, function and esthetics (9, 10), with particular concern for the relation of the lower part to the cupola (never resolved to the full satisfaction of architects and consultants). The idea of a pure form resting on the ground was not possible here because to house 2,500 seated persons would have meant too large a building, overwhelming in the city and on the skyline. Belluschi paced off gas tanks and reservoirs to see how so large a structure would look and decided on the base as a necessary compromise. (Another cathedral, Kenzo Tange's St. Mary's in Tokyo, uses a warped surface "dome" without a base but this is a much smaller building, seating only 800 with standing room for 1,000 more, with traditional nave and sanctuary—as different from St. Mary's San Francisco as any two Gothic cathedrals are from each other.)

The final design—St. Mary's today—is both dramatic and serene. It is "no mere neutral design," nor does it depend on "engineering tricks" or on "archaic architectural terminology," all of which the Archbishop proscribed. The shells of the cupola, unique on the skyline, announce a building whose purpose is distinct from that of other buildings, as he asked. But the interior is the true glory of the cathedral, the justification of the exterior. All the effort and agony of creation in an age of technological and sociological complexity find their recompense here, where the clarity of the idea is fulfilled. In the single space created by the cupola, rising 190 feet from the floor, is the message of today's church: oneness, integrality, unity; of sanctuary and nave, of priest and people, of all men with each other.

The two great works of art which are themselves at one with the building are the brilliant stained glass windows 6 feet wide by 130 feet long, designed by Gyorgy Kepes for the junctures of the hyperbolic paraboloids along the sides and overhead; and Richard Lippold's shimmering baldacchino of aluminum rods, suspended from the cupola by slender gold wires, with a simple gold cross at its center. No lesser quality of design in whatever works of art are yet to come will be worthy of the building.

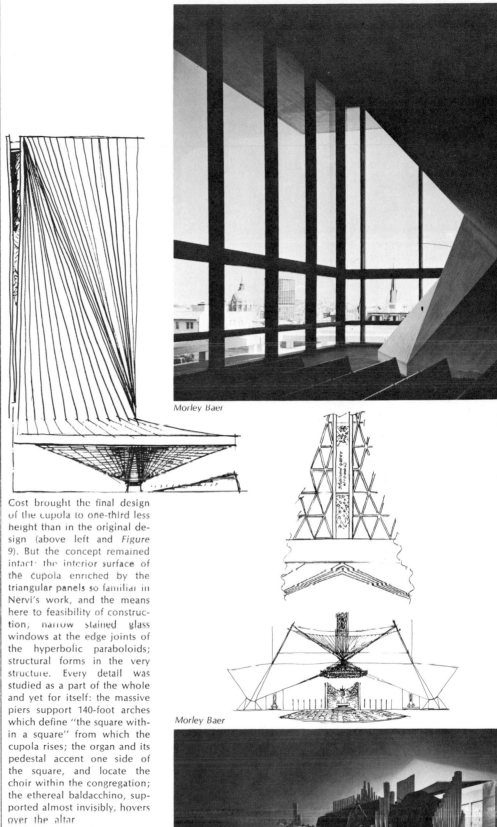

Morley Baer

Morley Baer

Cost brought the final design of the cupola to one-third less height than in the original design (above left and Figure 9). But the concept remained intact: the interior surface of the cupola enriched by the triangular panels so familiar in Nervi's work, and the means here to feasibility of construction; narrow stained glass windows at the edge joints of the hyperbolic paraboloids; structural forms in the very structure. Every detail was studied as a part of the whole and yet for itself: the massive piers support 140-foot arches which define "the square within a square" from which the cupola rises; the organ and its pedestal accent one side of the square, and locate the choir within the congregation; the ethereal baldacchino, supported almost invisibly, hovers over the altar

SAINT MARY'S CATHEDRAL
Morley Baer

Morley Baer

Predella, altar and pulpit, with the simple rosewood reredos, are surrounded on three sides by seats, none of which is farther than 100 feet away.

SAINT MARY'S CATHEDRAL, San Francisco, California. Architects: *McSweeney, Ryan & Lee—William Schuppel*, project architect; *Michael Kelly*, project coordinator. *Pietro Belluschi*, consulting architect, design. Engineers: *Leonard F. Robinson & Associates*, structural; *Woodward-Clyde-Sherard*, soils; *Keller & Gannon*, mechanical/electrical; *Dariel Fitzroy*, acoustics; *Seymour Evans & Associates*, lighting. *Pier Luigi Nervi*, consulting engineer, design. *Auguste Raes*, acoustical consultant. Landscape architects: *John H. Staley & Associates*. Artists: *Gyorgy Kepes*, stained glass; *Richard Lippold*, baldacchino. Contractor: *Cahill Construction Co.*

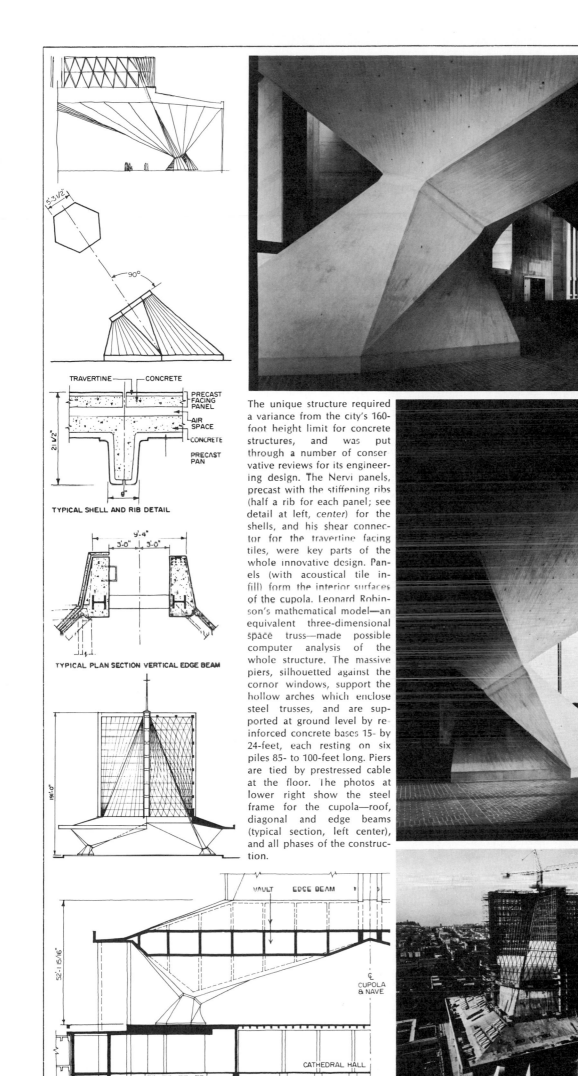

TYPICAL SHELL AND RIB DETAIL

TRAVERTINE — CONCRETE

PRECAST
FACING
PANEL

AIR
SPACE

CONCRETE

PRECAST
PAN

TYPICAL PLAN SECTION VERTICAL EDGE BEAM

VAULT   EDGE BEAM

CUPOLA
& NAVE

CATHEDRAL HALL

DRILLED PIPES

Morley Baer

Morley Baer

The unique structure required a variance from the city's 160-foot height limit for concrete structures, and was put through a number of conservative reviews for its engineering design. The Nervi panels, precast with the stiffening ribs (half a rib for each panel; see detail at left, *center*) for the shells, and his shear connector for the travertine facing tiles, were key parts of the whole innovative design. Panels (with acoustical tile infill) form the interior surfaces of the cupola. Leonard Robinson's mathematical model—an equivalent three-dimensional space truss—made possible computer analysis of the whole structure. The massive piers, silhouetted against the corner windows, support the hollow arches which enclose steel trusses, and are supported at ground level by reinforced concrete bases 15- by 24-feet, each resting on six piles 85- to 100-feet long. Piers are tied by prestressed cable at the floor. The photos at lower right show the steel frame for the cupola—roof, diagonal and edge beams (typical section, left center), and all phases of the construction.

Paul S. Kivett photos

Congregation B'Nai Jehudah

THE NEW SANCTUARY FOR CONGREGATION
B'NAI JEHUDAH
Kansas City, Missouri
Architects: *Kivett and Myers*
engineers: *Bob D. Campbell & Company
(structural), Richard Bradshaw (consultant), W. L.
Cassell & Associates (mechanical and electrical),
Bolt Beranek and Newman, Inc. (acoustics);*
contractor: *Sharp Brothers Contracting Co.*

*A remarkably effective religious atmosphere has been created in this Sanctuary
addition to the Temple B'nai Jehudah complex in Kansas City. The original buildings, designed by Kivett and Myers about twenty years ago, included facilities for a
small chapel, religious education classrooms, administrative offices, and a large
social hall serving many functions, including banquets, meetings and musical concerts. The new Sanctuary, shown here, was designed in deliberate contrast to the
other facilities—a separate space used only for worship and with a character that
clearly states this.*

*The Sanctuary evokes one of the oldest structural forms, the tent, but trans-
lated into today's materials and methods. And the interior, punctuated by an 83-
foot-tall concrete center pole, provides a big, serenely uncluttered space perme-
ated by soft blue light from the spiraling plastic skylight. Sparkling within this quiet
atmosphere are the bronze forms of the Ark, the Menorah, the Eternal Light and
lettering for the Ten Commandments—all designed and built by Norman Brunelli,
Kansas City artist and sculptor. Both the shape and lighting of the interior keep the
eye focused on the altar and its furnishings; the rest of the space is kept very simple. A curtained-off area behind the Sanctuary can be opened to provide a considerable amount of added seating when needed. Fabric panels are continued around
to the altar to unify the area visually and to help the acoustics.*

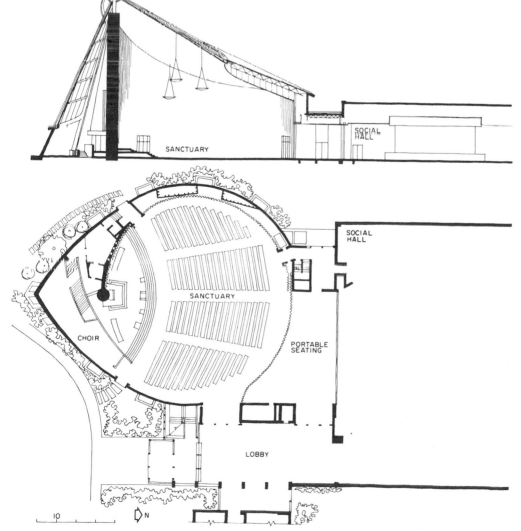

To create the desired visual dominance of
the complex, the new Sanctuary differs
not only in its strong shape, but in basic
materials: the older units are brick, while
the exterior supporting walls of the new
structure are bushhammered concrete. Interiors
are finished in plaster, exposed concrete and
drapery. The building, containing 30,000 square
feet, was inexpensivley built. The curtained-off
expansion area can be noted in plan and the photo
below.

To avoid any possible glare from the attention-
holding skylight, the plastic panels
are of a translucent, deep-colored blue
which transmits a minimum soft-hued light
(photo, page 100).
They are hung below the steel frame. The
structural system provides an uninterrupted
open space for a congregation of 1000.
In spite of its drama, the basic success of
the space is its straightforward simplicity
in the use of materials and finishes, leaving
the religious symbols to stand in high relief.

The major portion of the roof area is supported by 5-inch tubular cables hung from the concrete mast. The roof structure itself is of two parts. A rigid conical helix of about 6 to 8-foot maximum depth is formed of straight joists; space within contains air ducts and electrical and mechanical systems. The outer conical shape is formed of 5-inch tubular steel. Nine post-tensioned, tie-down cables stabilize eccentric loads, and are anchored 30 to 45 feet deep into bedrock ledges.

Tuskegee Chapel

The Tuskegee Chapel at Tuskegee Institute in Alabama, a 2000-student Negro college may be one of Paul Rudolph's most significant works. Designed in collaboration with the firm of Fry and Welch (both black architects), it is an outstanding, original and remarkably effective religious building. It possesses the symbolic power of Le Corbusier's Ronchamp — acknowledged by Rudolph as a source — and is clearly influenced by Wright, especially inside. The ideas of Corbu and Wright, however, have been transformed by the architect's creative imagination to achieve a unique and highly personal work of art.

Because the Christian faith has been and will continue to be the major ideological force behind the founding and growth of this interdenominational school, and a major historical force behind the black man's struggle for equality in the United States, a strong sense of rightness made the administrators of Tuskegee wish to replace their old chapel, struck by lightning and burned to the ground in 1957, with the finest church they could afford by the best architect they could find. Unfortunately, because their fine new chapel has been built for and by Negroes in the deep South, many

observers will be tempted to see qualities in the church which evoke the Negro struggles in a literary way—to see the building, for example, as a walled, windowless fortress open only to the sky and sheltering its occupants from a hostile environment.

Such fantasies, while understandably comforting to some, miss the point. The highly abstract forms of the Tuskegee chapel are universal symbols, relevant to all Christians. Rudolph's chapel, given a similar site and program, would be as right for Harvard as for Tuskegee, and this is as it should be.

The chapel is the focal point of the campus and has been constructed near the site of the burned-down church it replaces. The photographs show the principal entrance located at the top of a broad ridge which runs through the center of the older part of the campus near the graves of Booker T. Washington and George W. Carver (the former the first principal and guiding force of the school, and the latter its first great scientist). This part of the school grounds still bears handsome traces of the original landscape plan by Frederick Law Olmsted, the first "advocacy planner" whose concern for the cause of Southern blacks began in his youth before the Civil War and continued throughout his career.

The roof of the chapel slopes boldly upward on its long axis, as at Ronchamp, and beneath its broad overhang the outdoor pulpit juts assertively forward in vertical space, just as it does on that famous French hilltop. The church was originally designed to have poured-in-place concrete walls supporting a hyperbolic paraboloid roof of open-web steel joists. To lower costs, the walls were redesigned as steel frames supporting brick cavity walls. The light-pink mechanically-produced brick lacks the character of the handmade bricks in the early Tuskegee buildings, which were molded by student bricklayers and fired in their own kilns, but it is as appropriate to the highly sophisticated building it sheathes as the handmade bricks are to the humbler structures which surround it.

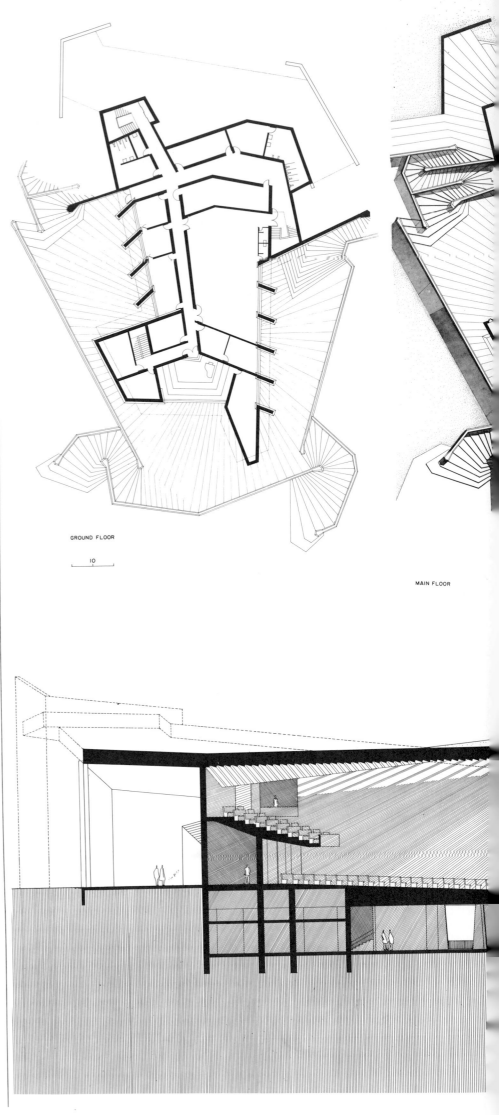

GROUND FLOOR

10

MAIN FLOOR

Rudolph's project drawings show the design as approved by Tuskegee's board of advisors on architecture. This board was formed by Moreland Griffith Smith, noted churchman, civil rights activist and architect, who in his role as consultant to Dr. L. H. Foster, president of Tuskegee, is the man principally responsible for bringing architects and planners of first rank to the school.

These drawings were made before the change from concrete to brick, but the finished building as a spatial concept is basically unchanged.

The photos on page 106 have been made from the downhill side of the ridge. Continuous brick surfaces bend and fold to form a sacristy and the real wall of the choir. A vertical surface perforated with openings which slant outward and are sealed with colored glass forms one wall of the meditation chapel. A rectangular surface perforated in the same manner brings shafts of light to the main stair. The sections (right) show the warped surface of the hyperbolic paraboloid roof which is formed by closely spaced open-web steel joists.

The chapel has been designed to function as a concert hall for the famous Tuskegee Institute Choir. The auxiliary spaces of the building will be used by the Tuskegee music school, until this entire sector of the campus becomes an art and music center, as part of Rudolph's new master plan for the campus.

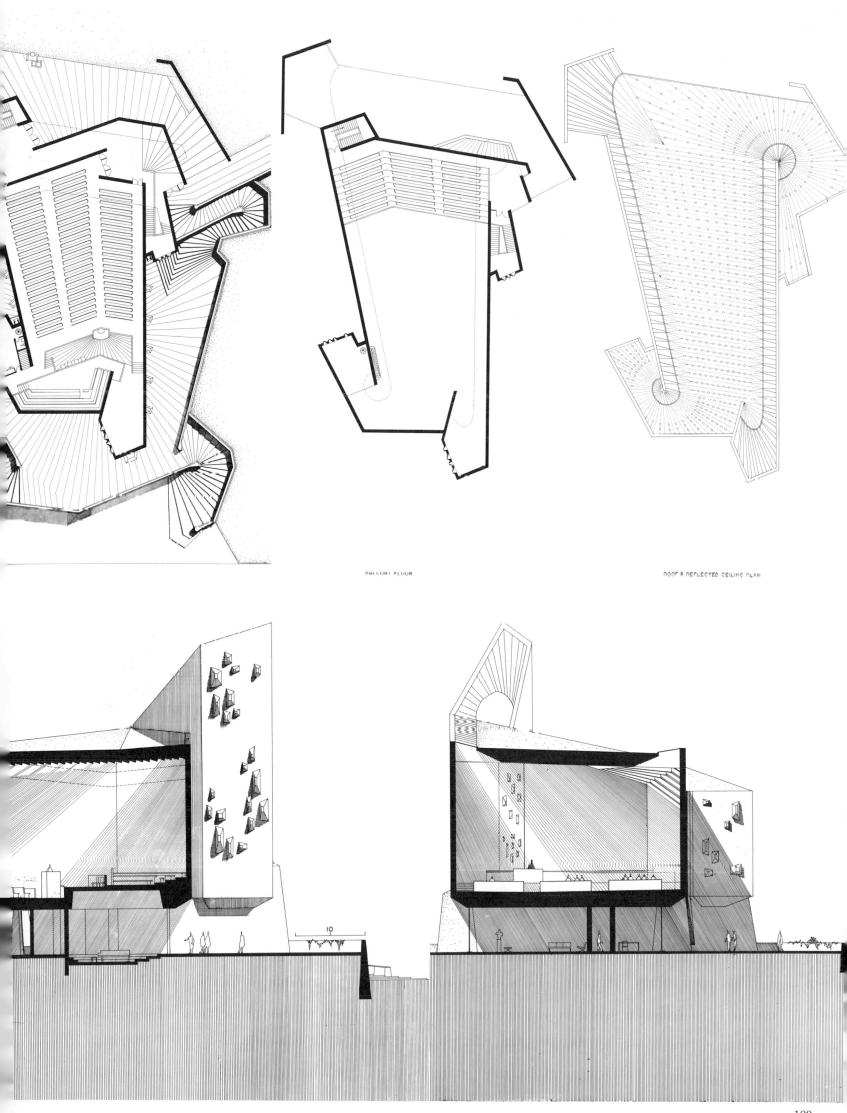

BALCONY FLOOR

ROOF & REFLECTED CEILING PLAN

10

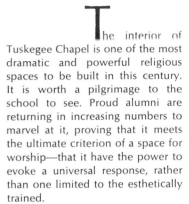

The interior of Tuskegee Chapel is one of the most dramatic and powerful religious spaces to be built in this century. It is worth a pilgrimage to the school to see. Proud alumni are returning in increasing numbers to marvel at it, proving that it meets the ultimate criterion of a space for worship—that it have the power to evoke a universal response, rather than one limited to the esthetically trained.

One approaches the interior from humble spaces—up the stair near the meditation chapel, or from the modest narthex—and suddenly enters a great asymmetrical room. The ceiling is marvelous—a great plane, curving in two directions, its warped surface formed by standard joists with straight bottom chords which appear to curve. The accordion-shaped plaster ceiling painted blue has been carefully engineered as a reflecting surface to enhance the acoustics. Air supply is equally distributed by means of brick-sheathed ducts on both sides of the chapel—handsome forms which complicate, yet enhance the interior space. Skylights parallel to the wall planes provide a mysterious and beautiful light.

The influence of Wright upon Rudolph is quite clear in this great room, but the architect appears to have drawn upon and transformed other sources of inspiration, including—unconsciously perhaps—certain images from German Expressionist films.

The views on pages 110–111 are of the chancel, the lower photograph having been taken from the balcony. The chancel has been designed to emphasize the importance of the Tuskegee choir, and will eventually have an organ on the rear wall. The dominant position of the pulpit expresses the importance of the Word. A minister who has preached in this 1,100-seat chapel reports that from the pulpit it has a quality of intimacy and that the congregation seems near.

Beyond the steps in the photo at left is the meditation chapel, a tall, narrow room illuminated by skylights and through colored glass set in deep reveals high in the wall.

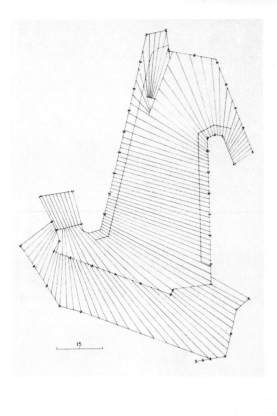

Le Corbusier said that the roof of Ronchamp was inspired by the shell of a crab which he found on a Long Island beach.

As the beautiful roof framing plan (immediate left) clearly shows, the spiral forms of the Tuskegee Chapel also appear to have been suggested by a creature of the sea. The rather less poetic diagram at the left and the early construction photos below show how this beautiful form was actually framed.

The structure is in some ways simpler and in other ways more complicated than it appears to be now that it is finished. The length of each open-web joist differs, and each slants at a slightly different angle to form the warped plane. There are 117 such members, not counting the slanting girders which carry them, and they weigh 71 tons. The columns also are of widely varying lengths.

The structure was complex enough to require much on-site measuring time by the fabricator to insure a minimum amount of field work. Since no two adjacent joists are parallel, temporary bridging was used for an initial line-up and permanent bridging custom fabricated and fit on the site. According to the American Institute of Steel Construction, the fabricator underestimated his engineering and drawing costs, overestimated fabrication costs and came out on target.

The top photo was taken from a position to the right of the great entrance porch and shows almost the entire roof including the final spiral rising to form the meditation chapel. The lower photo shows how the roof curves downward across the chancel toward the sacristy, and how it rises on one side and descends on the other as it approaches the narthex, the entrance vestibule and the main stair.

TUSKEGEE CHAPEL, Tuskegee Institute, Tuskegee, Alabama. Architects: *Fry & Welch, Architects & Planners;* associate architect (design phase): *Paul Rudolph;* architectural consultant for campus: *Moreland Griffith Smith;* structural engineer: *Donald J. Neubauer;* mechanical engineer: *A. Dee Counts;* electrical engineers: *Frank J. Sullivan Associates;* acoustical consultant: *Bolt Beranek and Newman;* contractors: *George B. H. Macomber Company and F. N. Thompson, Inc.*

Chapel
of the Assumption

This is a small Roman Catholic chapel which is located in a cemetery just south of the city of Medellín in Colombia. According to the architects, the motivating concept of the design here was a desire to express the Christian hope of the resurrection of the body and life after death in terms of a clear and dramatic structural shape for the building. So a structural system was devised, using two triangular frames that rise to a height of over 90 feet above the chapel's altar. These in turn support 52 white concrete ribs which spring up to reach it and which have infill of gray-tinted glass. Since the ribs spring from the perimeters of a plan that is rhomboidal, the resulting three-dimensional shape becomes complex and remarkable, as it creates an interior space, brilliantly lit, that rises upward from a relatively low entrance portal to its full height above the altar. The interior modifies all of this drama somewhat with a touch of austerity, in that, aside from the altar itself, there are no other furnishings. The basement of the church contains a crypt and a small chapel, and there is also a ceremonial platform at the main entrance for funerals.

CAPILLA DE LA ASUNCION, Medellín, Colombia. Architects: *Laureano Forero and Rodrigo Arboleda.* Engineer: *Jaime Muñoz Duque (structural).* Consultand: *L. and L. H. Forero (landscape).* General contractor: *Arquitectos Ingenieros Asociados Con-Con-Creto.*

St. Francis de Sales Church

Hedrich-Blessing photos

St. Francis de Sales Church in Muskegon, Michigan, recently completed by architects Marcel Breuer and his partner Herbert Beckhard, is a major work of religious architecture which exhibits great technological daring and expressiveness. In explaining their approach, the architects assert their belief that a high degree of architectural imagination is still appropriate to religious forms. Says Breuer: "How much this building affects those who see and enter it, how much it signifies its reverent purpose, will depend on the courage its designers manifest in facing the age-old task: to defeat gravity and to lift the material to great heights, over great spans—to render the enclosed space a part of infinite space. There the structure stands—defined by the eternal laws of geometry, gravity and space." To achieve their aim Breuer and Beckhard chose a geometry of hyperbolic paraboloid side walls, parallel at their base to the long axis of the nave. As these planes complete their rotation they resolve into backward tilting trapezoidal end walls, perpendicular to the nave axis. The broader of the two, shown in the photograph at the right, occurs at the juncture of the nave and the low mastaba-like narthex. Designed to receive the side walls, it is wide at the top and narrow at the bottom. At the sanctuary end, the reverse occurs. There the trapezoid is smaller, and appropriately narrow at the top to sharpen the focus on the altar.

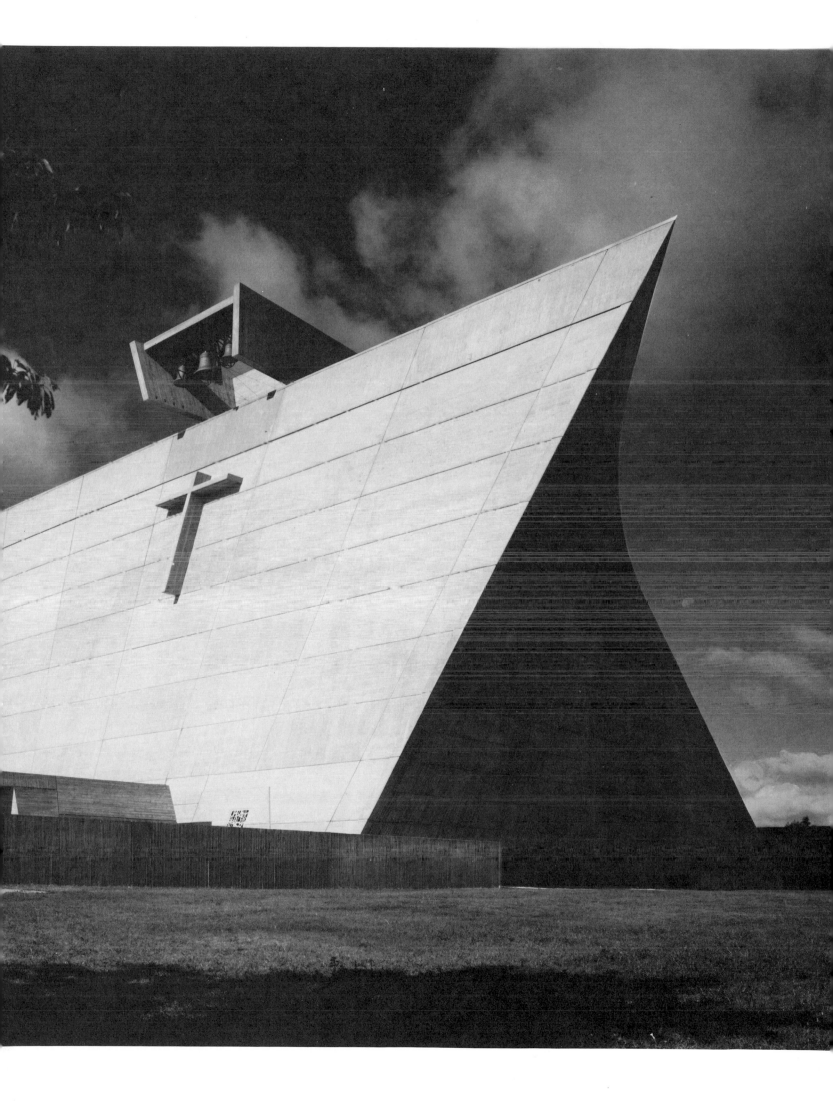

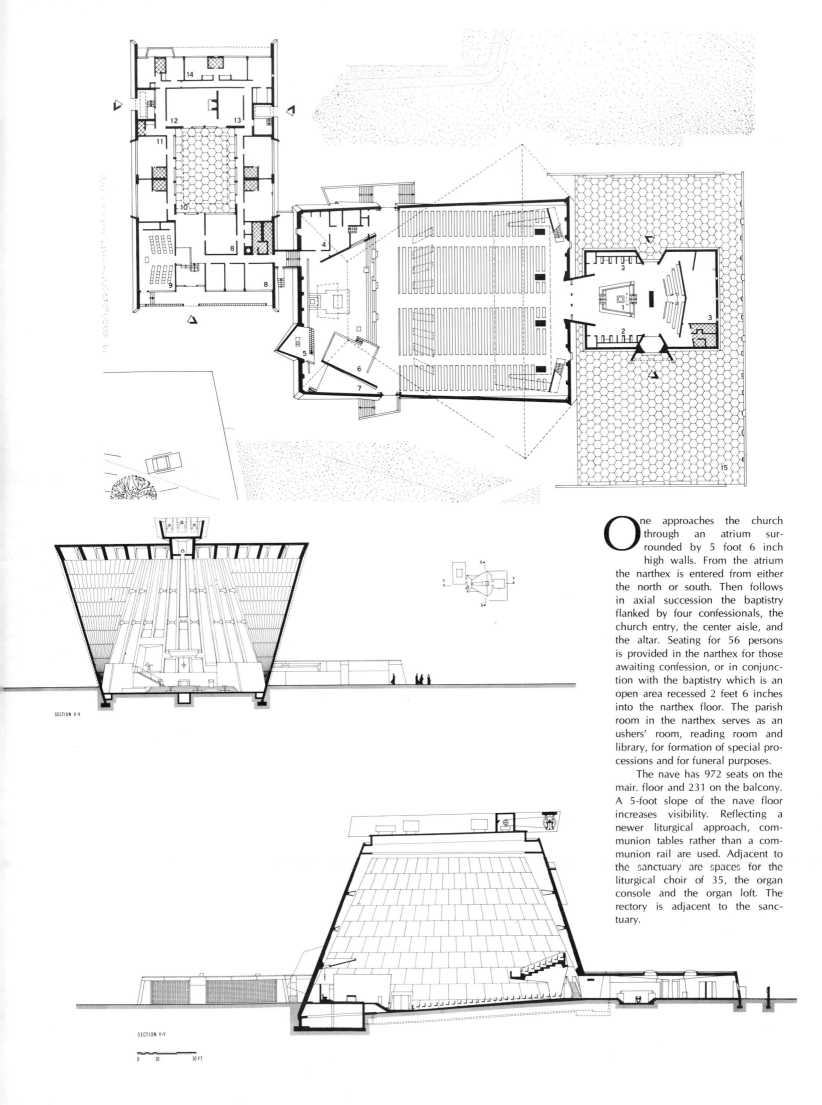

SECTION X-X

SECTION Y-Y

0   10   30 FT

One approaches the church through an atrium surrounded by 5 foot 6 inch high walls. From the atrium the narthex is entered from either the north or south. Then follows in axial succession the baptistry flanked by four confessionals, the church entry, the center aisle, and the altar. Seating for 56 persons is provided in the narthex for those awaiting confession, or in conjunction with the baptistry which is an open area recessed 2 feet 6 inches into the narthex floor. The parish room in the narthex serves as an ushers' room, reading room and library, for formation of special processions and for funeral purposes.

The nave has 972 seats on the main floor and 231 on the balcony. A 5-foot slope of the nave floor increases visibility. Reflecting a newer liturgical approach, communion tables rather than a communion rail are used. Adjacent to the sanctuary are spaces for the liturgical choir of 35, the organ console and the organ loft. The rectory is adjacent to the sanctuary.

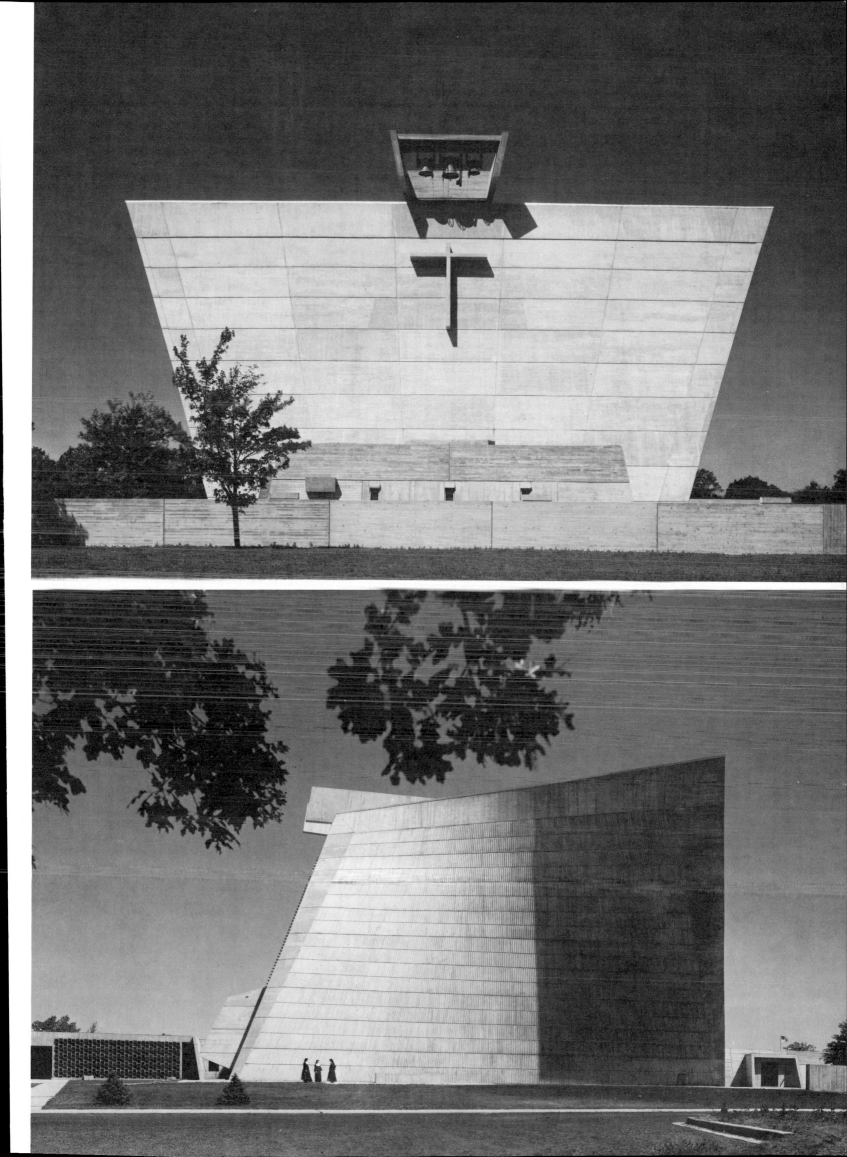

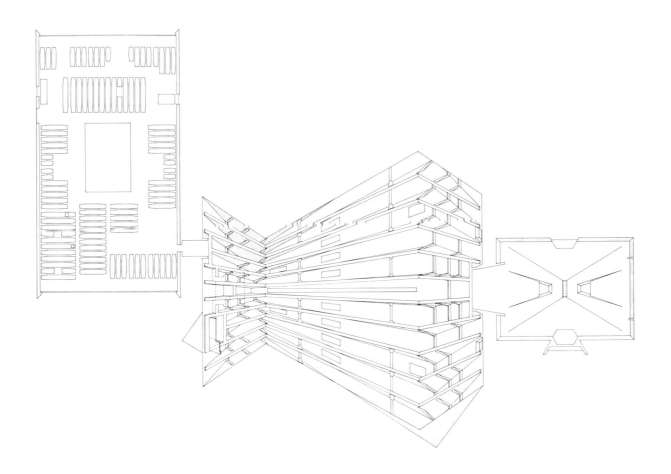

The 75-foot-high structure is topped by a concrete trough which houses the suspended bells. It also contains ventilating equipment. Natural light is introduced to the nave by means of skylights while artificial lighting originates from a special lighting slot running the length of the roof. Indirect lighting from behind the sanctuary screen walls and the back of the balcony augments this system. A rather unusual feature of the sanctuary is the chapel for the Blessed Sacrament. It is elevated from sanctuary level so that it may be seen from all points. The celebrant faces the congregation and his chair is behind the altar. By means of lighting control either the main altar or the chapel becomes the focus of attention. The church space is spanned by means of a system of rigid concrete arches connecting three trapezoidal planes: the front wall, the rear wall and the roof. The hyperbolic paraboloid sidewalls are self-supporting, enclosing the space and stabilizing the structure. The balcony is a free-standing element in the nave supported and cantilevered from four columns located so as not to interfere with the visibility of the sanctuary from any seat. Both narthex and rectory have loadbearing exterior walls.

E xterior surfaces are architectural concrete. The bold texture of the warped sidewalls was created by formwork composed of regular boards of constant dimension distributed on a surface of double curvature, as shown in the diagram below.

St. Francis De Sales Church, Muskegon, Michigan. Owner: *St. Francis de Sales Parish—Reverend Louis B. LaPres, pastor.* Architects: *Marcel Breuer and Herbert Beckhard;* structural engineer: *Paul Weidlinger;* mechanical engineers: *Stinard, Piccirillo & Brown;* acoustical consultants: *Goodfriend Ostergaard Associates;* lighting consultants: *Svend W. Bruun;* general contractor: *M. A. Lombard & Son Co.*

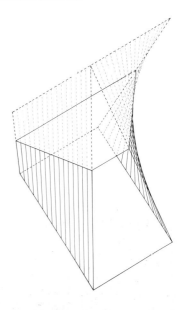

Temple Beth El

In striving to create a worthy interior space for a new sanctuary
for Temple Beth El in West Palm Beach, architect Alfred Browning Parker
used the qualities of structure as his chief means of expression. The form—
what Parker calls a "spiraloid"—swirls gracefully upward, culminating
in an impressive clerestory window. The calm magnitude of the
interior space enhances the religious experience and the inherent
characteristics of the form give the exterior an arresting appearance.

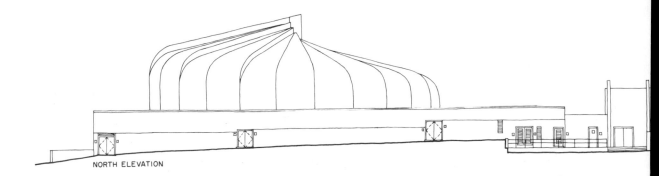

NORTH ELEVATION

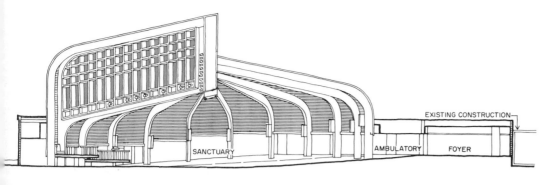

This sanctuary for Temple Beth El is the new focal point and unifying element of an existing complex of social hall, chapel, classrooms and administrative offices for a Conservative Jewish congregation.

A significant volume of space is created in the circular sanctuary by 24 exposed laminated wood arches (spaced at 15-degree intervals) and ascending like a spiral staircase to a height of 51 feet 10 inches. The arches are locked together at the apex by a steel cylinder 4 feet 6 inches in diameter and 26 feet 8 inches deep, which acts as a compression ring.

The bema (the raised platform from which services are conducted), and the ark (the cabinet containing the Torah) are traditionally located on the eastern wall. The impressive clerestory window is positioned overhead, admitting natural light from the south to illuminate the bema and the ark. The window is 20 feet 6 inches by 49 feet 10 inches, segmented by a laminated wood framing system. Around the circular sanctuary but open to it is a low ceiling "ambulatory space" for circulation and extra seating. This smaller-scale space and the classroom/office building are concrete.

According to the architect, the design was inspired by, but is a stylized version of, the shell of a marine mollusk—the chambered *Nautilus pompilius,* whose coiled shell is segmented internally. "I wanted to create an aura of ascending space while utilizing the engulfing atmosphere of the circle," says Parker. "A special interior space must exist in religious buildings, a space that is functional but is in itself an inspirational element."

The regular seating capacity is 800 in a fixed, semi-circular arrangement allowing as many people as possible to be near the bema. The unusually large ambulatory can be converted into temporary seating for 400 on the High Holy Days.

A limited budget necessitated the selection of wood for the sanctuary, instead of concrete (the material originally considered); as well as the standardization of elements (including the arches), and fast, efficient on-site erection of the shell.

FREAD SANCTUARY, TEMPLE BETH EL, West Palm Beach, Florida. Architects: *Alfred Browning Parker, Architects.* Engineers: *Jorge Peña y Lillo* (structural), *Hufsey-Nicholaides Associates, Inc.* (mechanical/electrical). General contractor: *Butler & Oenbrink, Inc. Lawrence Galloway, project superintendent.*

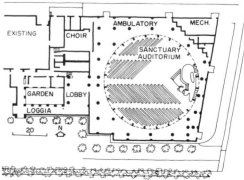

Alfred Browning Parker, Architects designed the copper light fixtures (which emit light from both the top and bottom) mounted on each arch, the ark, the almemars (pulpits), Menorah (candelabrum) and the Eternal Light hanging above the bema. There is no other art work except the Hebrew characters located on the exterior near the entrance.

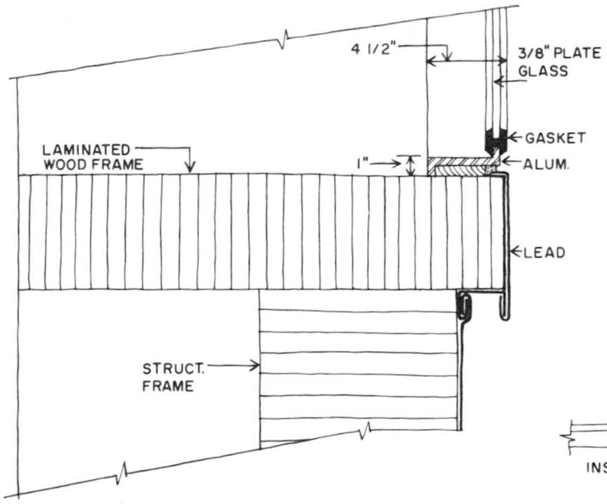

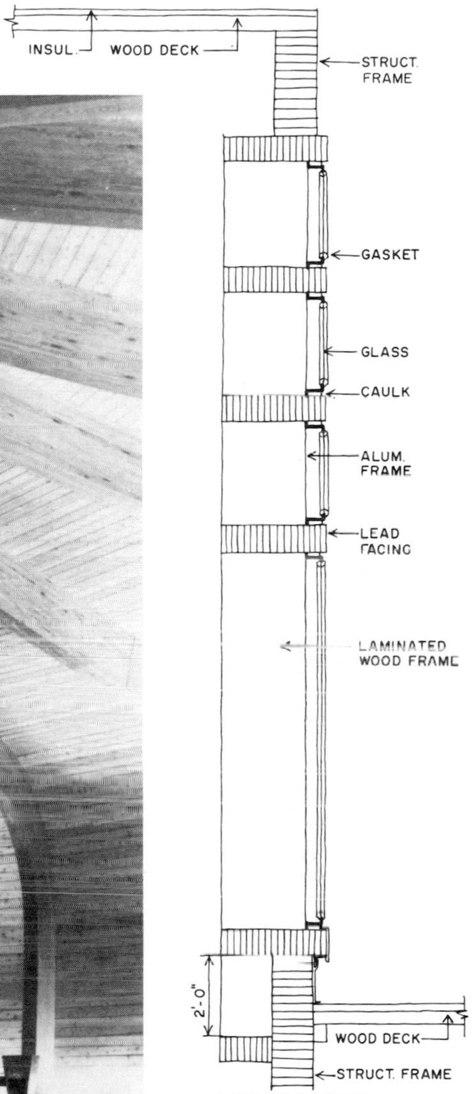

4 1/2"
3/8" PLATE GLASS
GASKET
ALUM.
LAMINATED WOOD FRAME
1"
LEAD
STRUCT. FRAME

INSUL. WOOD DECK
STRUCT. FRAME
GASKET
GLASS
CAULK
ALUM. FRAME
LEAD FACING
LAMINATED WOOD FRAME
2'-0"
WOOD DECK
STRUCT. FRAME

SECTION THROUGH THE GREAT WINDOW

Exposed arches and cedar walls form one continuous, sweeping interior line from floor to ceiling apex. The arches are of pine and roofed by heavy wood decking with a cedar finish. Color was added by a subdued orange-colored carpet and varying shades of rose-colored material on pew seats, the brightest shade nearest the bema. The dominating clerestory window is segmented by laminated wood members that are secured with visible steel clips.

127

CHAPTER SIX:

FITTING INTO THE LANDSCAPE

What is the advantage of attending a temple or church away from the crowded city? The view, of course, and the uncluttered space that just might prolong a mood of prayerful contemplation or communal harmony after you've stepped outside the house of worship. Most of the buildings in this chapter were constructed on rolling hillsides in such a way that they complement an already lovely site. A quietness of design prevails, imitative of the surrounding landscape.

An important part of integrating church into hillside (or mountainside) is the choice of materials. These churches, whether built of natural materials or of concrete or steel, reflect the tone and texture of their backdrop. Lafayette-Orinda's timber-framed roof fits into the hilltop with a delicate subtlety; and even though the interior houses a large space and congregation, the scale of the building makes no attempt to dwarf the individual or to compete with the surrounding landscape.

The Memorial United Methodist Church in Avon, Connecticut, built of concrete, has as its main interior feature a shaft of natural light cast from the skylight onto the altar. The forms of the church's bell tower and roof seem to imitate the incline of the sloping hills around the site. Next to the stunning Santa Monica mountains, the Stephen S. Wise Temple, in its use of natural and warm color, confirms the solidity of the building in its own right.

Roger Sturtevant photos

Lafayette-Orinda United Presbyterian Church

The hilltop location called for the strong and simple form of this church, clearly announcing the nature of the building and fitting in agreeably with the beautiful landscape that is its backdrop. In form and scale the building relates to the residential community which surrounds it, but in volume it is large relative to the congregation it serves, a design approach evolved from an observation of the architects: that the impact of a large space is lasting and requires no face-lifting to renew itself. The great timber-framed roof with its many small members, the wood plank walls, and the refinement and precision of details close at hand bring the scale of the great interior space into relation with the individual. The shape functions well acoustically for both musical sound and for the spoken word.

LAFAYETTE-ORINDA UNITED PRESBYTERIAN CHURCH, Lafayette, California. Architects: *Burton L. Rockwell* and *Richard Banwell*. Engineers: *Nicholas Forell & Associates*, structural; *Smith & Garthorne*, electrical; *Kasin, Guttman & Associates*, mechanical; *Dariel Fitzroy*, acoustical. Landscape architects: *Royston, Hanamoto, Beck & Abey*. Stained glass design: *Mark Adams*. Contractor: *C. Overaa & Co.*

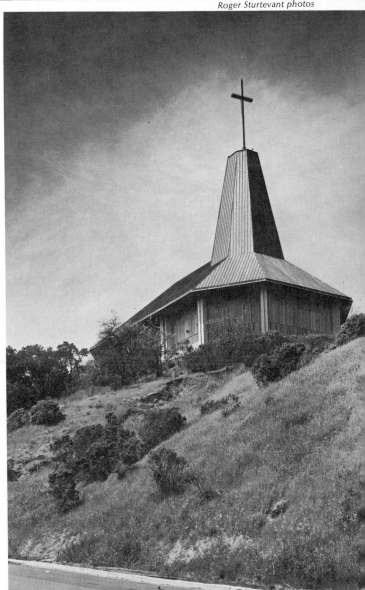

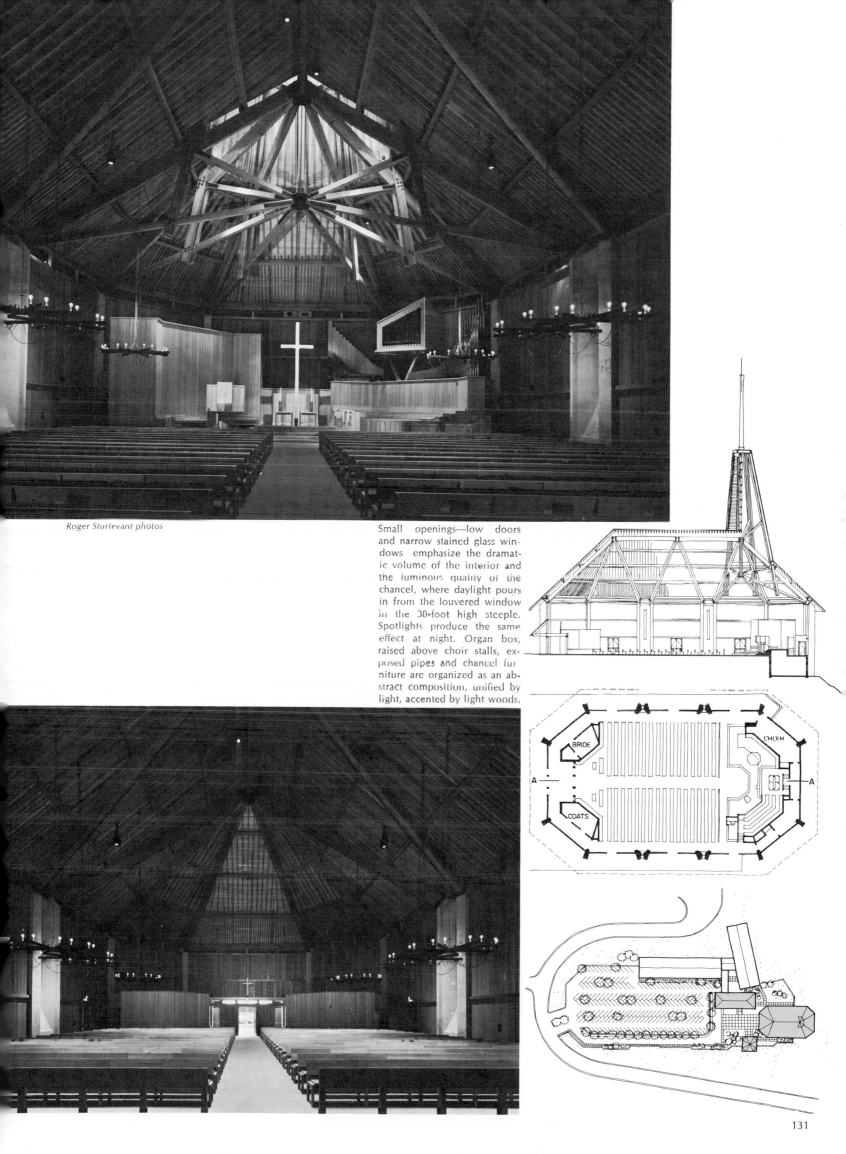

Roger Sturtevant photos

Small openings—low doors and narrow stained glass windows emphasize the dramatic volume of the interior and the luminous quality of the chancel, where daylight pours in from the louvered window in the 30-foot high steeple. Spotlights produce the same effect at night. Organ box, raised above choir stalls, exposed pipes and chancel furniture are organized as an abstract composition, unified by light, accented by light woods.

Stephen S. Wise Temple

The Stephen S. Wise Temple in the Santa Monica Mountains above Bel Air, Los Angeles, houses a variety of facilities for congregational activities but the organization of its plan and its elegant design give it an air of essential simplicity, strong and positive in its own right.

Jordan Lagman photos

KIT.

NURSERY

SANCTUARY &
SOCIAL HALL

ADMIN.

CR.

CR.

CR.

CR.

N

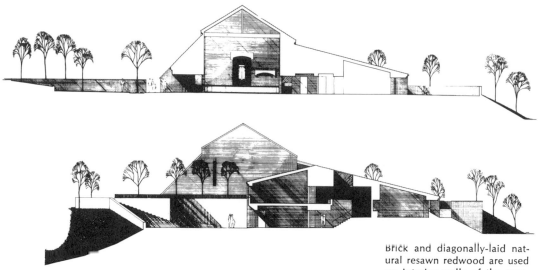

Brick and diagonally-laid natural resawn redwood are used on interior walls of the present sanctuary, and are the principal materials in the semi-enclosed court between classroom wings. Classroom structures are framed in natural concrete. The tile-covered roofs (below) slope to the playing fields on the south side of the complex.

This tranquil temple complex, with its variety of facilities in the tradition of Jewish religious buildings, is located on a site in the Santa Monica mountains with a superb view which gives no clue to the proximity of the site to the Bel Air section of Los Angeles. Careful grading provided locations for the several elements of the complex without changing the natural variation in levels. The building—it is actually one building, disposed so that each of its parts has, in effect, an identity of its own—is on four levels: sanctuary level and the three levels of the religious school. The various elements are tied together by the handsome brown concrete tile roofs whose elegant profiles are a strong aspect of the character of the complex.

The complex presently consists of the sanctuary, offices, school, nursery and two playing fields, but this is just part of a master plan which eventually will provide a permanent sanctuary northeast of the driveway circle, a chapel, and outdoor amphitheater and additional space for offices and classrooms. The present sanctuary will then become the social hall and multi-purpose room. A small university is to be built on the adjacent site, forming an unusual center for religious and intellectual study. The entrance to the present complex is level with the parking areas, and overlooks a great court of irregular shape with spectacular views to the mountains. The monumental steps leading down to the court and its outlook make it an exceptional gathering place for outdoor events. At one side of this court is one of the two two-story classroom wings; it is separated from the other wing by a semi-enclosed court. Seven rectangular wells, whose size and depth vary with the mass of the roof structure, admit daylight to the court which serves as entry for both the offices and the class-rooms, and connects by stairway with the sanctuary.

The character and quality of this building derive from its architect's sure sense of form and knowing use of materials. In essence it is a simple building, though its functions are multiple, but it is never stark. The choice of materials, and their handling, and the limited palette of colors and textures, contribute to this quality. Materials are natural and warm in color: red-brown face brick, natural resawn redwood siding, board-formed concrete left natural, laminated wood beams, brown concrete tile, dark-brown painted wood and metal trim.

STEPHEN S. WISE TEMPLE, Los Angeles, California. Architects: *Daniel L. Dworsky & Associates.* Engineers: *Erkel, Greenfield & Associates,* structural; *Takahashi, Tobian & Horiuchi,* mechanical; *Saul Goldin & Associates,* electrical. Landscape architect: *Emmet Wemple.* Contractor: *Conant & Lieberman.*

Otto Baitz photos

Memorial United Methodist Church

The congregation of this church approached their architect with a strong and well-defined program, a minimal budget, and a magnificent site of four acres in a pasture with views of rolling wooded hills. The fundamental principle of the building program was that the life of the church begins in worship, and a second tenet—almost immediately as important—was that for the uses of tomorrow as well as today, a flexibility had to be built into the design for worship. Seating was required for 240 people, including a choir of 30, and supplementary seating for special services needed to be able to be brought in (from a storage room off the narthex, as it turned out). The resulting church is a structure of considerable simplicity, made of concrete block bearing walls. As is so often the case in contemporary churches, natural light—shown above—is used to denote the altar, the focal point of the whole building; here the clerestory that admits a sheet of light at that point is almost the only "architectural" feature of the interior, and it gains enormously in power for that. Outside, the angular, fragmented shapes of the block suggest, without copying them, older church forms.

MEMORIAL UNITED METHODIST CHURCH, Avon, Connecticut. Architects: *Philip Ives Associates—associate-in-charge: Edward W. Winter.* Engineers: *Throop & Feiden (structural); I. M. Robbins (mechanical/electrical).* General contractor: *Fred Brunoli & Sons.*

Jo Alexander

River Road Unitarian Church

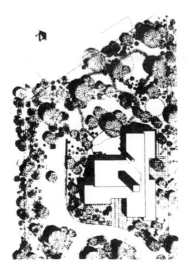

This Unitarian church conveys the atmosphere of a religious building without structural gymnastics or elaborate transliterations of historical forms, and its unforced simplicity is highly appropriate to the intellectual religious philosophy it houses. The character of the site, a wooded knoll in a suburb of Washington, D. C., was an important design influence. The fact that the congregation elected to build the major portion of the program at once meant that architects Keyes, Lethbridge and Condon could place the church in such a way that the mass of the auditorium is offset by that of the two-story classroom wing, located a half-level above and a half-level below the floor of the meeting room itself. The church thus becomes a very close part of its hillside site and forms a unified composition that reads as a single building. Parking and access roads have been sensitively sited, and all new planting was chosen to preserve the character of the existing landscape.

J. Alexander photos

Above: porch leading from the auditorium. At right: part of the sequence of entrance spaces. Below: steps leading to the main entrance. Smaller steps at far right lead to the church office.

RIVER ROAD UNITARIAN CHURCH, Bethesda, Maryland. Architects: *Keyes, Lethbridge & Condon;* structural engineer: *Robert A. Weiss;* mechanical engineers: *Kluckhuhn & McDavid Company;* landscape architect: *Lester A. Collins;* general contractor: *Furman Builders.*

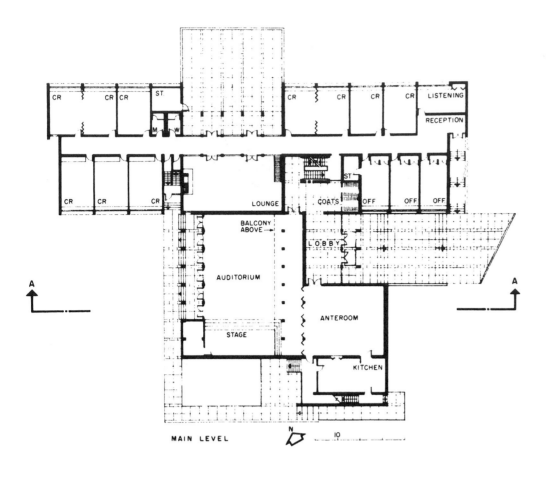

MAIN LEVEL

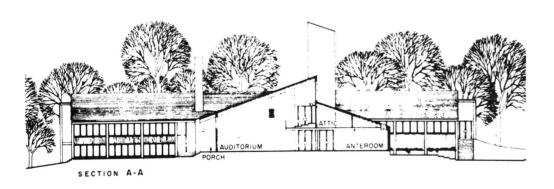

SECTION A-A

Coming through the main entrance to the church, the arriving members of the congregation find themselves in a story-and-a-half space whose ceiling slopes up, away from the door. Turning to the right, they next enter a continuation of the same space, except that it is now deeper, so that the roof goes up high enough for there to be a balcony underneath it. Those entering the main auditorium will walk under the balcony and turn to the left, those bound for the gallery will go up a double flight of stairs—situated within the bell tower and thus a narrow shaft of space—and then come back across the balcony and straight into the gallery of the church.

The structure combines steel, brick bearing walls and wood, with the major spaces being taken in steel, which is partially cased in wood. Light entering the clerestories is controlled by fixed wood louvers. White-painted brick, natural wood finishes and ochre paint are used throughout the church.

Bethlehem Lutheran Church

Relocated from downtown Santa Rosa, when a redevelopment project encroached on its existing building, to a six-acre suburban site where it could serve a growing neighborhood, Bethlehem Lutheran Church is both traditional in feeling and non-traditional in form. The triangular plan with its four banks of pews (instead of the more usual two) derives from the program requirement that the congregation have the sense of gathering around the altar without actually doing so. The tetrahedral form of the building is a direct reflection of the plan, but is appropriate to the building's location on the crest of a hill surrounded by other hills. The simplicity and directness of the pyramidal form, broken only by the skylight, satisfied both the congregation's request for a simple form and the architects' hope that they could provide a building of timelessness. The cedar-shingled roof does not reach to the ground but stops short above glass walls on the perimeter. Inside, the frame is exposed and redwood boards fill in between bents. A single chandelier is used for primary lighting of the building. The organ is behind the altar. Thanks to the sloping site, the choir room could be located below the chancel. Freestanding redwood "boxes" at the entrance provide a "crying room" and storage space. Originally, the program called for separate buildings for sanctuary, parish hall and Sunday school. The final plan put parish hall, Sunday school and offices in one building made up of 25-foot modules.

BETHLEHEM LUTHERAN CHURCH, Santa Rosa, California. Architects: *Duncombe/Roland/Miller.* Engineers: *Forell-Elsessor-Chan* (structural); *Harding-Miller-Lawson* (foundation / soils); *Marion, Cerbatos and Tomasi* (mechanical/electrical). Contractor: *Todd Construction Company.*

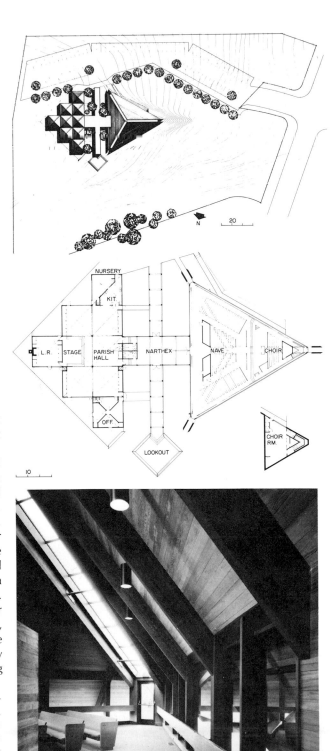

Jeremiah O. Bragstad photos

143

Although the altar is on axis with a central aisle in a traditional relationship between chancel and nave, the seating arrangement suggests a less formal relationship and gives the sense of closeness to the altar that the program required. A bank of low windows on the perimeter admits natural light.

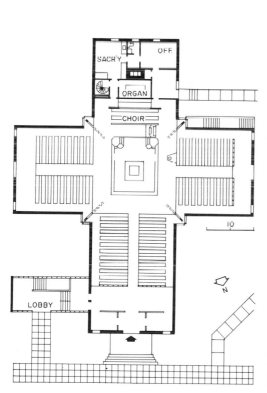

St. Barnabas Episcopal Church

The design of this delicate, gently scaled, and specially lighted Episcopal church was only one part of an over-all study which was undertaken by the architects. The new church was to be constructed on a softly rolling site in suburban Delaware, and the entire complex was intended eventually to include a large church school as well as a sanctuary proper and rooms for other more directly liturgical activities. The new school still is waiting to be built, but its anticipation is reflected in the prominent entrance lobby to it, which is located just left of the main entrance to the church itself. This lobby now contains as well a flight of stairs that lead down to classrooms and an assembly hall below the existing church.

The most striking feature of the interior of the church is a large double cross, so designed as to be visible from all sides, and made of stained glass. This hangs above the main altar, and it is lit from skylights above, in the roof of the crossing of nave and transcept. The interior supports for the crossing also become, outside, the church's spire, in a lacy web of structural elements topped by a cross.

ST. BARNABAS EPISCOPAL CHURCH, Marshallton, Delaware. Architects: *Victorine and Samuel Homsey.* Engineers: *Victorine and Samuel Homsey (structural); Ewald and Miller (mechanical/electrical). Double cross above the altar designed by June Groff.* General contractor: *W.D. Haddock Construction Company.*

CHAPTER SEVEN:
FITTING INTO THE CITYSCAPE

A keen sense of urban planning characterizes all the buildings in this chapter. We witness the challenge of the architect faced with two problems: serving the needs of the congregation, and dealing with the givens of the dense urban landscape. These two factors, interconnected, lead the architects to some outstanding solutions.

In the case of Safdie's very special project in Jerusalem, his ambitious task was to tackle a project directly tied into the Holy City's overwhelming history. In discussing the problems encountered while rezoning the Western Wall and building a new yeshiva, he asks: "Can one create a contemporary vernacular and reestablish the basic values of this environment? Can one build continuity from the old to the new? Can one unite the scales of all life's activities? It seems, here in Jerusalem — the city of all men, a place of holiness, of love and longing — that to mend its scars and restore its vitality might be the fulfillment of a dream of reconciliation for all mankind."

Hugh Stubbins' goals for St. Peter's Church, compared with Safdie's sense of mission, sound more down to earth, but just as difficult. Stubbins had in mind to instill St. Peter's with hospitality, using the church as a catalyst for the community to use the space surrounding the new office building. This spirit of hospitality resembles that expressed in St. Thomas Church where a placard in the vestibule reads: "Friend, there is a welcome in this Church for thee. . ." However, in St. Thomas's, hospitality is restricted to the interior, and its success depends on its ability to remain appropriate in scale to the neighboring city block and street. Where St. Peter's has a clear view overhead and a comfortable feeling of open space, St. Thomas's bulk and mass distinguish it as an easy place to meet in the midst of Manhattan.

The other projects, Charles River Park Synagogue and the Ecumenical Center, seem to have opposing programs. The Synagogue contains the dignity of a religious building, set apart from the busy downtown area in which it is situated; while the Ecumenical Center successfully links ecclesiastical, university, and city dwellers through Fleischman's careful organization of space.

Charles River Park Synagogue

In the late 1950s, when urban renewal was still an acceptable euphemism for bulldozing, large areas of Boston's West End were condemned and cleared. Among the structures lost to this once thriving working class community was the old North Russell Street Shul—a synagogue that has served more than half a century as a center of worship for a 1500-member Orthodox congregation. After protracted court battles, the congregation finally received from the city compensation adequate to a new building program and commissioned Childs Bertram Tseckares Associates, Inc. to design the new structure shown on these pages.

The site selected is on Martha Road and is surrounded by towering blocks of apartments. To ease the transition between a busy downtown street and a sanctuary of quiet contemplation, the architects developed a series of interlocking screen walls at the entrance. These walls, in an act of architectural "decompression," deliver the visitor through a landscaped courtyard and into the building's entry vestibule. The main sanctuary which can accommodate 250 worshippers, is located under a sloping translucent ceiling that reaches a height of 25 feet at its upper end. A social hall, separated from the main sanctuary by a concealed sliding partition, satisfies the need for overflow space at special services or High Holy Days.

The 5000-square-foot building is faced with fluted masonry blocks both inside and out. The cambered, curving walls and self-conscious forms are designed to center attention on the synagogue itself and detach it visually from the massive rectilinear forms of surrounding buildings.

CHARLES RIVER PARK SYNAGOGUE, Boston, Massachusetts. Architects: *Childs Bertram Tseckares Associates, Inc.* Engineers: *Thomas Rona* (structural); *Samuel Ussia & Associates* (mechanical/electrical). Contractor: *Poley-Abrams Co.*

Ralph Hutchins photos

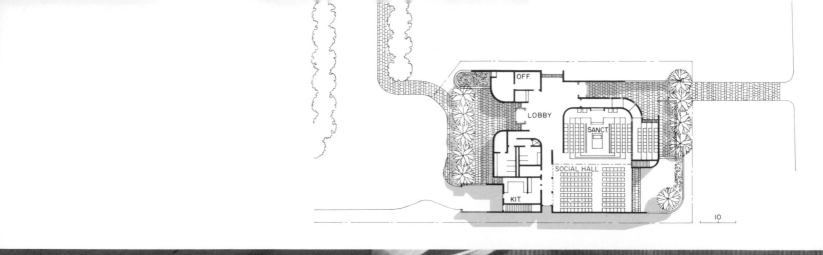

Following Talmudic tradition, the tablets over the ark (photos below and right) are square shaped and fashioned of stone from Galillee. The eternal light is contained in a black metal holder designed by the architects, and hangs over the tablets.

Photo (bottom right) shows a small ceremonial courtyard used in good weather for weddings and at Sukkoth, the fall harvest festival.

St. Thomas Church

One of the oldest traditions in architecture is tradition it-self—the use of understood and proven precedents which are partly repeated, partly modified to make a new building. No matter what they say, all architects rely on tradition. It may be an old one ("Georgian") or it may be fairly new ("Modern"), and it may even be the latest fad brought hot from the drafting room of a fashionable architecture school. But tradition won't be ignored, because a knowledge of what might be done under a particular set of circumstances—and how, in fact, it has been done—is too useful a tool of architectural practice, just as it is one of the cornerstones of architectural education. Such knowledge guides the architect through a bewildering variety of specific choices, emphasizing certain possibilities while giving others lower priority. Glass walls and exposed steel enclosing a rectilinear space, for instance, carry with them a host of suggestions for making the rest of the building, just as do walls of rough wood or shingles around a plan shot through with surprising diagonals. Traditions also conjure up images for both the inhabitant and the architect; they provide a set of alternatives for what a building might actually look like as well as how it can be formed. And a knowledge of what has been done in the past obviously avoids the useless reinvention of the wheel (happily leaving more time for those wheels that really do need reinventing).

Ralph Adams Cram and Bertram Goodhue, the designers of the 1911 St. Thomas Church in New York, paid notable attention to architectural tradition, and in fact they did so with so much erudition and scholarship that most of us now are likely to think of them as merely—to use that faintly derogatory word—"traditional" architects. St. Thomas Church certainly *looks* traditional, and people who remember it remember it most often for the abundance and elegance of its Gothic detail. Cram and Goodhue clearly understood the power that well-known architectural images have over the mind, and they knew just which set seemed appropriate in this case, and how to make them correctly. They also knew how traditional forms could be used to solve traditional problems like walling in an interior space and covering it over and lighting it.

It may therefore seem surprising that the building which resulted is in many ways boldly original, having finally about as much to do with real Gothic architecture as the town of Chartres with Manhattan. For Cram and Goodhue seem to have used Gothic precedent in a particularly creative way—not just to provide formal models for each of the parts and a controlling image for the whole, but as an indication of what was usual and what was unique about the design problem at hand. That is, if a tradition—any tradition—is taken as the framework for a particular design, then part of it will fit and part of it most probably will not, and will have to be modified. If, as in the case of St. Thomas Church, the chosen tradition has extensive associations, then the ways it fits and the ways it doesn't each take on an unusual importance. A building like St. Thomas Church thus speaks as vividly of the particular (this church in a modern city) as of the general (the Church). It is this combination of general and particular, abstract and specific, traditional and original—and not some elegant mode of architectural historicism—that makes the building worth revisiting in the aggressively un-Gothic late 20th century.

Ralph Adams Cram and Bertram Goodhue were partners in the firm of Cram, Goodhue and Ferguson of New York and Boston, and together they designed a number of important buildings in the early 20th century—most of them in Gothic style and most of them religious

(including the chapel of the United States Military Academy at West Point). Cram, like many other Gothic Revivalists in England and America, was grandiosely spiritual in his allegiance to the style, attaching to it an almost moral significance. So great was his fervor that he insisted, for instance, on building St. Thomas Church, except for the roof truss, entirely out of masonry in the traditional manner, without the aid of structural steel—though, due to a miscalculation, steel had to be added later to keep the north wall from collapsing. Goodhue seems to have been a little more easygoing in his approach, regarding Gothic as one alternative among many, rather than the ultimate way. When the firm of Cram, Goodhue and Ferguson was dissolved in 1914, just as the major part of St. Thomas Church was being finished, he went on to design buildings in various other styles, including the exuberantly "Spanish" theme building for the Panama-Pacific Exposition in San Diego and the starkly pre-Modern Nebraska State Capitol in Lincoln. Because Goodhue became one of the most original of the established architects in the early 20th century, and because part of the originality of St. Thomas Church consists of the bold and chunky massing characteristic of Goodhue's work, it is hard to resist thinking that he had the upper hand in the building's design, even though custom says otherwise, possibly because at the time the building was built Cram was the more fashionable architect.

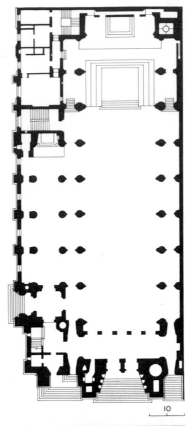

In any case, the design problem was this: how to provide seating for a large number of people (as well as space for offices and other parochial activities) on a relatively small urban site, and how to make a building that, from the outside, could remain a firm presence in the city even as its surroundings changed, as they inevitably must. The solution to the first part of the problem is straightforward if somewhat unorthodox; the main interior space of the building extends from virtually the front of the site to the very back, and it is shifted off center to the north, leaving just enough room for offices and a chapel with a gallery above on the south (53rd Street) side. The most memorable feature of the interior, which is otherwise dignified in a solid and rather plain way, is the enormous reredos above the altar at the (geographical) west end; it was designed by Goodhue and Lee Lawrie, a versatile artist who was also responsible for some of the best Art Deco sculpture in Rockefeller Center, and its ivory-colored stone contrasts with the warmer and darker sandstone of the rest of the interior. Though all of the figures conform to a carefully planned iconography, the reredos as a whole reads most strongly as a rich and delicate texture. In architectural terms the most instructive thing about it is that it is an object lesson in making virtue of necessity, for the sense of depth and lightness created by the multitude of niches and canopies in the reredos betrays the fact that, with the exception of three windows high above the floor, this end of the building is actually a blank wall that abuts the building next door, formerly a house and now the Museum of Modern Art. Similarly the north wall is blank, though that fact is obscured by the much more dominant clerestory windows set some ten feet back from the lot line, and identical to those on the south side of the nave. Thus there is a good deal of *seeming* here—architectural dishonesty, some would say—because what is in fact a symmetrical space set off center in an asymmetrical plan and walled in on two sides by adjacent buildings is made to feel central and unencumbered.

The asymetrical plan which is a peculiar feature of the interior also plays an important part in solving the second part of the design problem—making a building that can

hold its own in the changing urban scene. When seen in elevation or as in the large photograph on page 155, the façade of St. Thomas Church seems truncated and almost bizarre—two-thirds of a Gothic façade, consisting of a massive and rather stubby tower and a more delicately ornamented "central" portal and rose window. The building, of course, has almost never been seen this way, except by an architectural draftsman, or by an adventurous architectural photographer, and the knowledge that it would not be must certainly have been one of the justifications for designing it this way. Normally, when the façade is seen straight on, the observer is at street level and fairly close by; from this vantage the projecting portal with its deep-set doors and wide stairs dominates, obscuring the eccentricity of the rest. When the building is seen from any distance at all, it must be from some point up or down the avenue, and from such an angle the tower—which is designed for solidity rather than for graceful height, in what would be futile competition with its neighbors—becomes by far the most dominant element.

Why, nevertheless, does it make any sense at all to organize a building in this way, except for the fact that such an organization reflects to some extent the arrangement of the spaces inside? The answer to this question, insofar as it suggests a general attitude, has important implications for urban design, because, unlike many buildings, St. Thomas Church is not composed around itself, nor indeed is it composed with any detailed regard for its immediate neighbors (all of which, incidentally, have changed since the building was built). Instead the exterior of the church allies itself with the most basic and almost certainly the most permanent feature of its surroundings—the city block and the city street. The outsize proportions of the square tower make it seem to the eye to mark the corner of Fifth Avenue and 53rd Street as surely as it marks the corner of the building, and the rest of the façade, not stopped by a second tower on the north, makes a gesture of continuity with its other neighbors on this side of the block.

It is interesting to note that in the late 1950s the architects and owners of Canada House (now called the Mutual Benefit Life Building) paid careful attention to St. Thomas Church when they designed and built their new building immediately to the north on Fifth Avenue by echoing the church's color and by silhouetting it against a plain and windowless south wall. Such urban courtesy is certainly not to be discounted, since it is rare, but one can't help wondering whether or not in this special case, where the older building is so strong, such courtesy was even required—and whether in fact it would not have been better simply to respect the format of street and sidewalk and façade (as the St. Thomas Church does) rather than to set the building back behind a small plaza (which is what happened with Canada House). Perhaps the architects mistook the older building for an elegant curiosity to be treated with delicate respect, rather than a fundamentally urban piece of architecture able to hold its own among its neighbors, as long as they respected the same rules. This is a mistake that is easy to make, but it is worth correcting, because St. Thomas Church in its close allegiance to the structure of the city and in its manifest concern for the way a building is perceived by people (rather than for some abstract formal clarity in the architect's mind) tells of a kind of architecture that is radically different from much that we have become accustomed to.

ST. THOMAS CHURCH, New York, New York. Architects: *Cram, Goodhue & Ferguson.*

St. Peter's Church at Citicorp Center

There has been a Saint Peter's Church at the corner of Lexington Avenue and 54th Street since 1862. In 1971, Saint Peter's old church was sold to Citibank with the agreement that the Congregation could build a new structure on the same site. The lantern of the church (above) is at the upper plaza level. The sanctuary floor, however, is one story down, at the level of the lower plaza. The sanctuary is a magnificent surprise. Passers-by on Lexington Avenue look down and into it from a large window at the sidewalk. No one expects to suddenly come upon a church interior without actually entering a church—and many stop, look and find their way in. The church is almost always alive with concerts, jazz festivals, and religious services. Stubbins is responsible for the design of the church. The platforms, seating, and the altar and its fittings are the work of Vignelli Associates. The small chapel (below) has sculptures by Louise Nevelson.

Back in 1970 Hugh Stubbins wrote to Henry J. Muller, a former vice president of the First National City Bank, which now calls itself Citibank. In his letter he set forth some of his first thoughts about what was then known as the office building/church project. Said Stubbins: "The new, slick, slab buildings that march up the avenues of New York and other U.S. cities are symbolic expressions of the Machine. They are anonymous—cool and inhumane. We must use the resources of big business, reinforced by moral and social ideas, to develop a new generation of office buildings planned for the community and expressive of the humanity of the individuals who use them. By revitalizing urban development with an emphasis on people, we could produce a more enjoyable place in which to live and work. Such a building might even be a source of inspiration for other cities.

"With the church as catalyst and the bank as supporter, we can design a new kind of place which all kinds of people will want to enter and become part of. While the church must have its own identity, I like to think how it could be enhanced and magnified if we combine it with a new kind of office building. I think furthermore that we should be able to see into the church from the outside, to see what is going on, be attracted and become part of it. There is a spirit stirring at Saint Peter's Church that could become a bright light in Manhattan."

From the beginning, the pastor of Saint Peter's, Ralph E. Peterson, knew what he and his congregation wanted the new church and Citicorp Center to be. In addition to serving the spiritual needs of the congregation, the church was to be a place of hospitality for anyone who wished however briefly to join in its activities. And he wanted the Citicorp Center environment to be as hospitable as his church. And so Peterson, like Stubbins, had much to do with persuading Citibank/Citicorp to develop an active marketplace combined with plazas for relaxation at the foot of its tower.

Norman McGrath

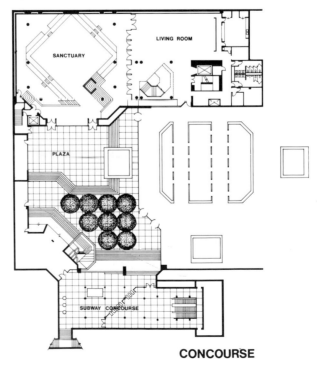

CONCOURSE

TWO JERUSALEM PROJECTS

Yeshiva Porat Yoseph

The Jordanians destroyed many of the numerous synagogues and rabbinical seminaries of the Jewish Quarter in the 1948 War of Independence and razed most of the rest of them during their 19-year occupation—after they had driven out the sector's tiny civilian Jewish population to be evacuated to Israeli-held West Jerusalem.

Since the Jews reclaimed their sector along with the rest of the Old City at the end of the Six-Day War, the Municipality of Jerusalem and the Corporation for the Development of the Jewish Quarter have been intensively rebuilding it. The most notable structure to be constructed so far is the nearly completed Yeshiva Porat Yoseph (below and right), a rabbinical college and Sephardic synagogue. Paid for in part by U.S. Jews and matched dollar for dollar by the Israeli government, it covers the site of the old Yeshiva which went up in flames in May 1948. Since Safdie was already at work on the Yeshiva when he was invited to design the Western Wall

Precinct, he has had a unique opportunity to bring the two projects into harmony.

"From the outset," said Safdie, "I tried to design the building in such a way that it would form a continuous whole with the rest of the Old City, but I nevertheless wanted to use contemporary building methods with all their potential. The Jerusalem bylaws demand that all exterior building surfaces, that is, both walls and roofs, be built of stone. In order to resolve this dilemma, I chose a dual system for building. Ten-foot-thick stone walls enclose the site and define the major zones of the building. The stone walls carry all the continuous linear and vertical services within the structure as well as all the passages, staircases, and light shafts. Within the spaces created by the stone walls is a second and completely contemporary construction system of precast concrete arch segments. The precast element, 10 feet high and 10 feet in horizontal reach, can form rooms 20 feet, 40 feet, 60

feet, 80 feet, or 100 feet square. As the rooms become greater in area, they become higher."

The precast elements will have translucent plastic domes. The synagogue chamber within the Yeshiva will be lit by domes located above giant prisms, which will break the sun's rays into a full spectrum of colors.

View of the Old City from the Mount of Olives. The Yeshiva, hugging the steep cliff of the Jewish Quarter, appears just behind the El Aksa Mosque on Temple Mount. None of its translucent plastic domes are yet in place. The Western Wall Plaza, not visible, lies in the valley between the Jewish Quarter and Temple Mount. The Yeshiva dominates the Jewish Quarter and holds its own as a monument in relation to the Islamic mos-

ques. Yet with great subtlety it answers in the affirmative the fundamental question Safdie asks himself and becomes a part of the solution of the problem he has set for himself in Jerusalem. In contemplation of the terraced and domed houses of the Jewish Quarter, the splendid walls of Herod's Temple with the Islamic mosques above them and the Turkish city walls of Suleiman the Magnificent—places of living and worship on the scale of a

house, a temple, and a palace—Safdie asks: "Can one create a contemporary vernacular and re-establish the basic values of this environment? Can one build continuity from the old to the new? Can one unite the scales of all life's activities? It seems, here in Jerusalem—the city of all men, a place of holiness, of love and longing—that to mend its scars and restore its vitality might be the fulfillment of a dream of reconciliation for all mankind."

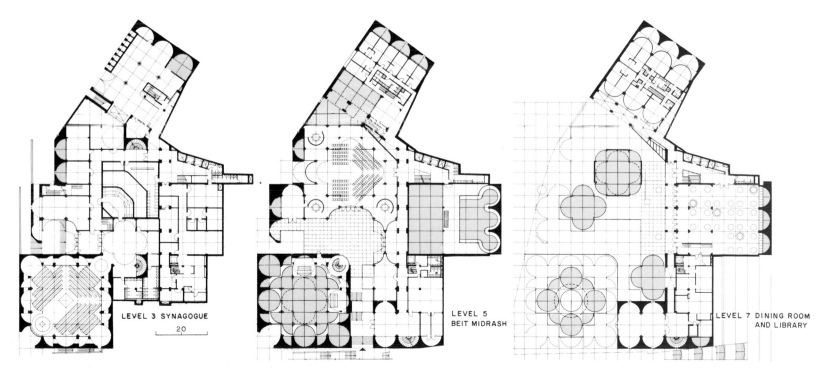

LEVEL 3 SYNAGOGUE
20

LEVEL 5 BEIT MIDRASH

LEVEL 7 DINING ROOM AND LIBRARY

Within the Yeshiva is a public synagogue for 400 people shown above in construction. Safdie, photographed on one of the Yeshiva's terraced roofs lives and works in Jerusalem and Montreal. The rabbinical students on the Yeshiva balcony can see Temple Mount, the Western Wall, the Old City walls and an Arab village (included in the picture) beyond. The steps adjoining the Yeshiva lead down to the Western Wall plaza.

Lee English photos

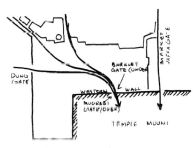

The pre-1967 condition
at the Western Wall

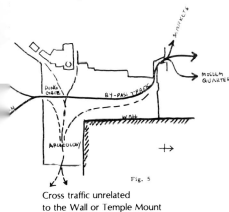

Pedestrian approaches
to the Western Wall Plaza

Pedestrian approaches
to Temple Mount

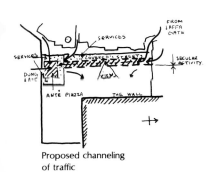

Fig. 5

Cross traffic unrelated
to the Wall or Temple Mount

Proposed channeling
of traffic

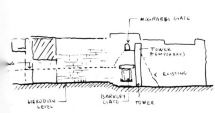

Elevation of the Wall

The Western Wall

In 1972, Israeli-born architect Moshe Safdie was commissioned by the Municipality of Jerusalem and the Corporation for the Development of the Jewish Quarter to devise a plan for the open space and adjoining neighborhood in front of the Western Wall in the Jewish Quarter of the Old City in East Jerusalem. It is the most holy of places for the world's Jews. Although Israeli leaders don't like to say so in public, the present setting for this monument does not meet their aspirations for the Jewish nation's most important Holy Place.

For centuries the Wall had been hemmed in by tightly interwoven small dwellings, some dating back to 1320, which were known as the Moghrabi Quarter. The little space used by the Jews who had come from distant lands to pray there is remembered as a narrow, shaded, intimate place only 40 feet by 120 feet, in which the Wall itself appeared to reach to the sky and the ancient stones seemed awesome, yet close.

Under Jordanian rule, only a few Jews among the tourists from Western countries had access to Judaism's most sacred place. Almost at the instant the Wall was liberated, the Israelis ordered that routes be cleared to the Old City by which every Jew in the world would come. Soon after, the Moghrabi Quarter was bulldozed to create a plaza large enough to contain the expected crowds. The space cleared measures 240 feet by 660 feet, not including the archaeological area to the south.

The Western Wall could now be seen from many angles and distances across the vast and dusty new square, but for many who remembered the Wall as it had been, it looked disappointingly different. It seemed diminished and, for some, less holy.

The sanctity of the Western Wall to Judaism arises from its nearness to the site of the Holy Temple of Solomon on Temple Mount at the heart of the Old City. The Wall itself is the southwestern portion of the rampart surrounding this ancient religious site which has been a great Islamic sanctuary (except for a Crusader Kingdom interval) from the 7th century to the present. Dominating the immense terrace of Temple Mount are the Mosque of Omar and the El Aksa Mosque, placed on axis with each other within a Moslem courtyard and garden surrounded by broad squares overlooking the Judean hills. Altogether they form one of the most beautiful architectural compositions in the world.

When Safdie began designing the forestage for the splendid backdrop of the Western Wall and Temple Mount, the square looked even worse than it had when the bulldozers finished, five years before. Since the site of the Old City of Jerusalem has been inhabited for at least four thousand years, archaeologists can't keep their hands off it, and the precinct of the Western Wall is one of their favorite digs.

By 1972 they had turned up four early Moslem buildings of the Omayyad Period (AD 660-750), including two palaces. Digging down layer by layer they had found Byzantine, Roman, Herodian, and pre-Herodian chambers and an Herodian street built shortly after 37 B.C. They had excavated to the foundations of the Old City wall built partly on Herodian and Mameluke remains by Suleiman the Magnificent from 1537-1541. They had exposed ten lower courses of the Temple Mount wall built by Herod. And much more.

The Archaeological Mission and Jerusalem's Mayor Teddy Kollek desired that some form of controlled public access to the sites be established.

The Western Wall Precinct is defined by the Wall itself to the east, the Old City wall and Dung Gate to the south, the Jewish Quarter rising steeply to the west, and the 14th-century Mahkamah building, sacred to the Moslems, to the north. Safdie began to plan the foreground for the Wall by selecting those existing streets, neighborhoods, gates and buildings which should—because of their historic importance, their beauty or their key location—influence his design.

The first of these is the Herodian street partially excavated by the archaeologists which borders the Wall and lies 30 feet below the level of the present plaza. This, he thinks, should become the lowest level of a new amphitheater-like plaza (section below).

The second is Barkley Gate (in sketch at bottom left), which was one of the principal entrances to the Herodian temple on Temple Mount. Presently unexcavated, it is located only a few feet above the Herodian street and connects through a 2,000-year-old underground stair to the courtyard of the Temple Mount. It could once more become an entrance, taking the place of the Moghrabi Gate above it.

The third element selected by Safdie as important to his design is Dung Gate—the only inelegantly named portal of the Old City's nine. The others, clockwise, are the Zion, Jaffa, New, Damascus, Herod's, Lion's, Golden and Sealed. Now the entrance closest to the Western Wall area from beyond the Old City walls, in Old Testament times it was the collection-point for the city's refuse. Safdie believes that the Dung Gate and its approaches should be transformed into a handsome and practical entrance to the Western Wall Precinct.

Since the plaza presently lacks toilets, first aid, restaurants, snack bars and tourist shops, Safdie's design calls for such facilities to be concentrated within a smaller plaza, immediately inside Dung Gate.

The fourth link between the Western Wall precinct and the rest of the Old City is the Arab market street, which forms a direct connection from Jaffa Gate to the narrow streets leading through the Jewish Quarter to the Wall. Finally Safdie has related his scheme to the 35-acre Jewish Quarter itself.

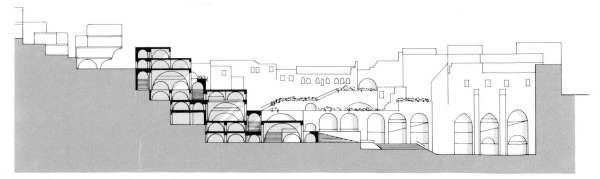

Toward the west of the proposed plaza and visible in the model photos (below) will be terraced institutional buildings forming the crown of the amphitheater. One of these is the Yeshiva Porat Yoseph (preceding pages) already nearing completion to the south. The architecture of the institutions and that of the terraces will be integrated in form and material so that there will be little demarcation between them. Safdie believes that the terraces will successfully

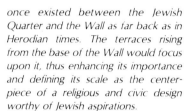

accommodate groups of different sizes. Small groups will assemble on the lowest level with a sense of intimacy and seclusion; larger groups will fill the successive levels rising upwards and each will have a good view of the Wall. The amphitheater form will restore the sloping topography which

once existed between the Jewish Quarter and the Wall as far back as in Herodian times. The terraces rising from the base of the Wall would focus upon it, thus enhancing its importance and defining its scale as the center-piece of a religious and civic design worthy of Jewish aspirations.

The design solution and its rationale

The Jewish Quarter is located upon a cliff parallel to the Western Wall about 30 feet above the plaza (top left). Safdie owns an 800-year-old house on the cliff edge of the Quarter and the view from his terrace (opposite page top) includes Temple Mount, the Western Wall and its plaza below. While designing the Wall's new foreground he has an ideal chance to observe how the present one works. He finds that the pilgrims form groups with different needs.

At times there are only a few people in the area privately praying and meditating as they seek closeness to the Wall. At other times groups of several hundred pray together or perform ceremonies. These need a separate area to enhance their group feeling and to keep them from disturbing the solitary worshippers. On great occasions—High Holidays or national mass rallies—tens of thousands of people gather together. They need to be able to see the Wall over each other's heads to strengthen their sense of where they are. The present plaza, since it is still an undesigned space meets none of these criteria.

Safdie proposes to excavate the present plaza down 30 feet to the Herodian level at the Wall. He will construct a series of terraces rising from this level to the crest of the Jewish Quarter to the west. These terraces, which will be widest near the Wall and become successively narrower as they step upward toward the Jewish Quarter, will form an amphitheater overlooking the Wall.

Photos courtesy Moshe Safdie and Associates

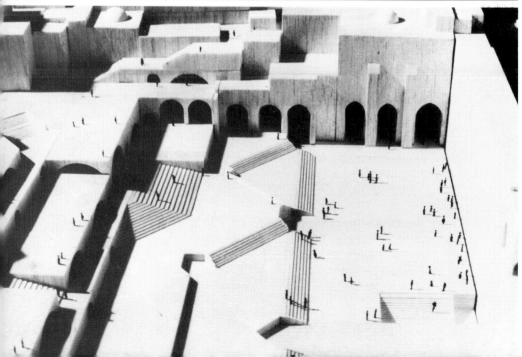

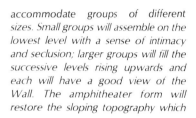

Safdie's amphitheater concept is an imaginative answer to the archaeologists' problem of how best to exhibit their findings to the public. It makes the most of the fact that various periods are found on different levels. Today's worshippers at the Wall stand on top of Omayyad, Byzantine, Roman, Herodian and pre-Herodian structures. Obviously these layers cannot be exhibited one directly on top of another period by period, nor each period be fully restored. Safdie propos-

es that portions of each excavated era be partially restored within the amphitheater terrace concept, with a terrace for each period. Thus the pre-Herodian and Herodian structures would be visited under the lower terraces. The visitor ascending to the middle terraces would find Roman and Byzantine restorations underneath. At a higher level, at least one Omayyad palace would be restored. The precise levels of the terraces would be established to accommodate the archaeologists' discoveries. Since the terraces gradually ascend to the cliff edge where the Jewish Quarter begins, they would unite the Quarter with the Wall in a dramatic and memorable way. The area available for public assembly in the Quarter would be greatly extended. Taking advantage of the amphitheater form, Safdie has designed several stately flights of stairs descending terrace by terrace from the main street of the Quarter to the Wall. One of the terraces will conceal an arcaded pedestrian street through which Arabs and others on their way to the Moslem market street by way of Dung Gate, can bypass the precinct of the Wall and the Jewish Quarter. This arcade would overlook the Wall

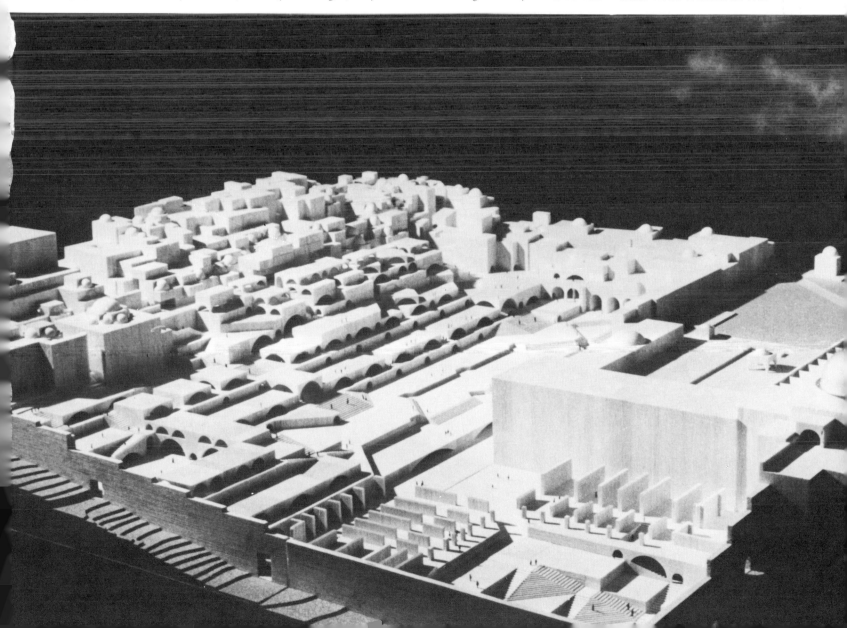

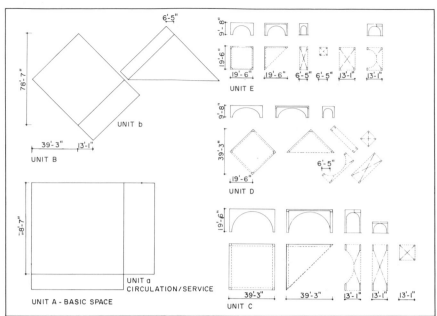

UNIT b

UNIT B

39'-3" 13'-1"

78'-7"

6'-5"

UNIT a
CIRCULATION/SERVICE

UNIT A - BASIC SPACE

8'-7"

9'-8"
19'-6"
19'-6" 19'-6" 6'-5" 6'-5" 13'-1" 13'-1"
UNIT E

9'-8"
39'-3"
19'-6"
6'-5"
UNIT D

19'-6"
39'-3" 39'-3" 13'-1" 13'-1" 13'-1"
UNIT C

Although old, handmade Islamic pottery, metalwork and textiles adorn his office and home, revealing a yearning love for the art of people who didn't know they were artists, Safdie's work is firmly anchored in the techniques of industrialized prefabrication and standardization for mass production. His love of handicrafts reflects his belief in the pre-eminence of craft, whether by hand or by machine. The Western Wall Precinct would be built of industrially prefabricated parts within the carefully worked out vocabulary of geometric shapes and sizes shown below. The Yeshiva Porat Yoseph (shown in recent construction photo on the opposite page) combines stone and concrete wall construction with an intricate system of modular precast concrete arch segments and plastic domes based upon the same geometric system.

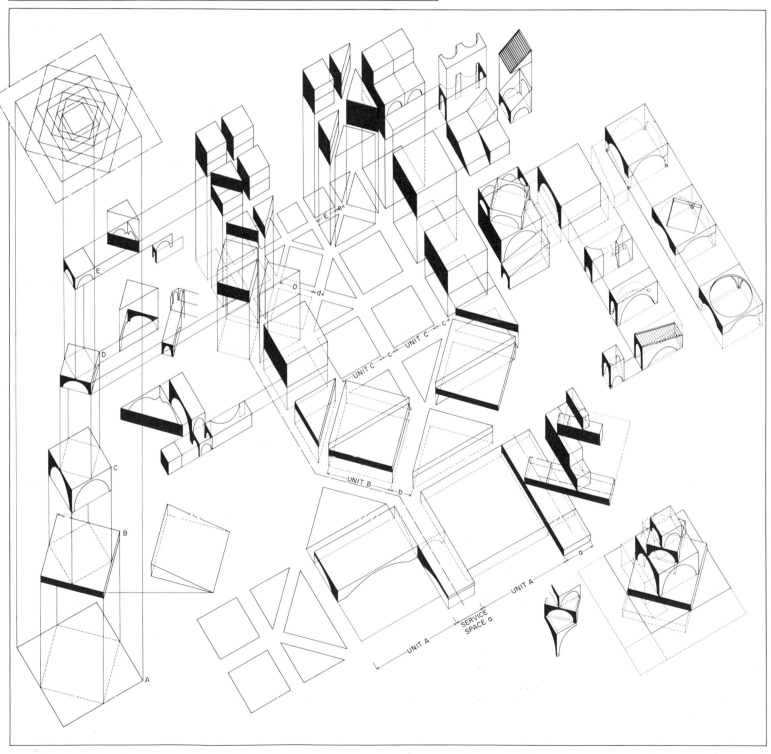

Watchtower Bible and Tract Society Dormitory and Classroom Building

Marko and Marko

The inclusion of three undistinguished 19th-century facades, behind which one half of this complex structure hides, might at first glance be dismissed as a quixotic attempt by Franzen to preserve the conditions of contradiction. In this case, however, the rules of the esthetic game were not established by the architect, but by New York City's Landmarks Preservation Commission. This body is empowered by the Landmarks Preservation Law to reject construction proposals which in its opinion will damage the appearance and quality of a so-called "Historic District." In turn the Commission is in an unique position to support construction which in its judgment helps maintain the character of the landmark neighborhood.

On December 1, 1965 the Commission designated Brooklyn Heights as New York City's first Historic District and earlier that year the Federal Government named it a national registered historic landmark. The Watchtower Bible and Tract Society, the official organization of the Jehovah's Witnesses movement, wished to build a 12-story dormitory and classroom building on the corner site which they presently own — shown in the photograph above opposite. A strong civic group, the Brooklyn Heights Association, supported by the New York City Commission, persuaded the Watch Tower officers to hire Ulrich Franzen to design a five-story structure more in scale with the residential quality of the old neighborhood. If the new building were to conform to present zoning codes, however, it would still be too high. The three facades are to be preserved therefore, not because anyone believes they have intrinsic architectural merit apart from their over-all scale, but because their preservation enforces a satisfactory height limitation on the adjacent structure, which is to be the first new project to be built in any officially designated landmarks district.

Use of brick, and break-up of the new building into elements of residential scale, keep it in harmony with the neighboring buildings.

WATCHTOWER BIBLE AND TRACT SOCIETY DORMITORY AND CLASSROOM BUILDING, Brooklyn Heights, New York City, N.Y. Architects: *Ulrich Franzen and Associates—associate-in-charge, Samuel E. Nylen.*

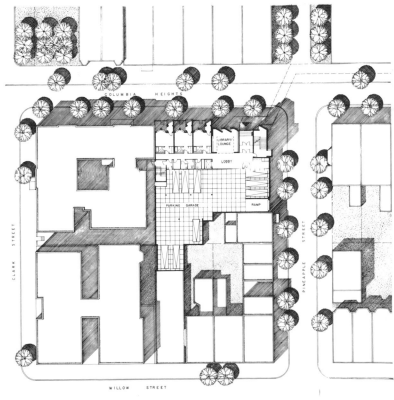

Ecumenical Center

Ten years ago, the University Circle Development Corporation initiated plans for a religious center on the Case Western Reserve University campus in Cleveland. The first buildings completed on the site were the Hillel Foundation, a Jewish center, and an addition, by Richard Fleischman Architects Inc., to the existing Church of the Covenant parish hall designed by Ralph Cram. Fleischman's addition consists largely of educational space—rather open in plan—for youngsters engaged in an ongoing program of religious education. Standing in forceful contrast to Cram's neo-Gothic structure, the new addition is expressed in sharply faceted forms of concrete and glass.

When these centers were operational, the Bishop of Cleveland commissioned Fleischman's firm to extend the ecumenical concept by designing a Roman Catholic center across the plaza and eventually to be known as the Hallinan Center. Two flexible areas were required in Hallinan Center: a large hall where Chaplain and students can meet to plan for worship, fellowship or related recreational activities and a small space to be used as a lounge and counseling area. The photo, page 170, shows the architect's solution with the small space on the balcony overlooking the larger space below. In contrast to the Church addition, the exteriors employ very extensive glazing to create a transparent quality from the plaza that, hopefully, acts as an open invitation to potential users.

The connective tissue linking all the buildings is a multi-leveled plaza, much of it designed by Fleischman's firm. It is free and playful in design, but reflects the diagonal geometry of the new buildings and expresses symbolically the important ecumenical character of the entire complex.

ECUMENICAL CENTER, Cleveland, Ohio. Architects: *Richard Fleischman Architects Inc.* Engineers: *Gensert Peller Associates* (structural); *Andrew Psiakis* (mechanical); *Ralph Linton* (electrical). Landscape architects: *John Litten & Associates.*

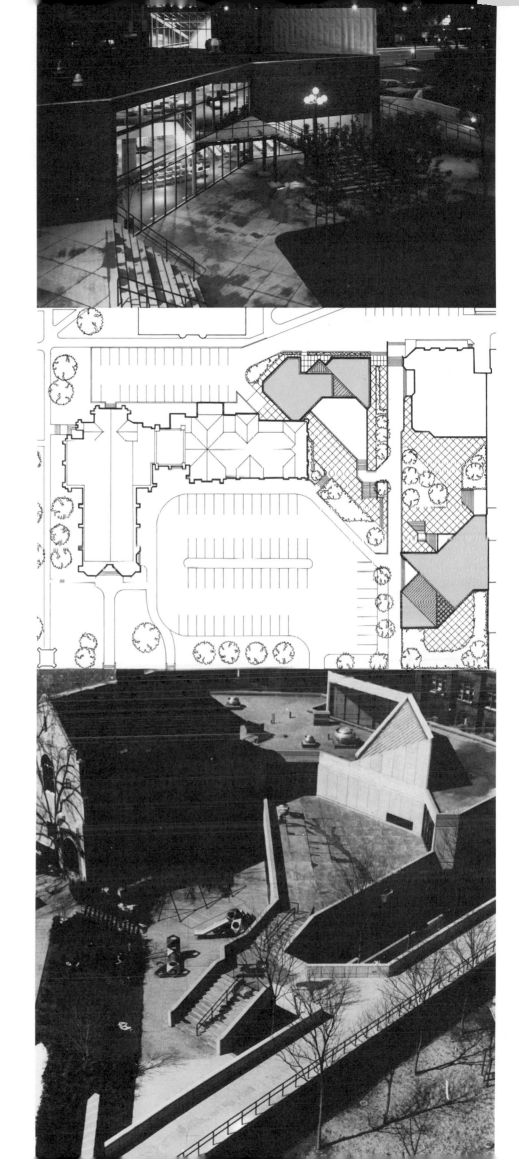

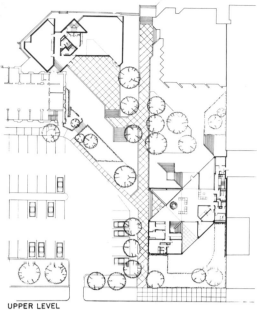

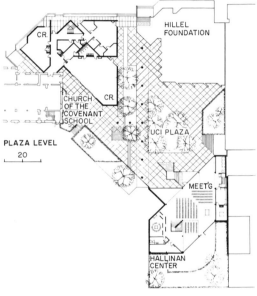

HILLEL
FOUNDATION

CR.

CHURCH
OF THE
COVENANT
SCHOOL

CR.

PLAZA LEVEL

20

UCI PLAZA

MEET'G

HALLINAN
CENTER

The angular geometry of the project
shows up most forcefully in plan. The
two Fleischman projects face each
other diagonally across the UCI Plaza.
The plaza has also become part of a
major pedestrian artery linking portions of the north and south campuses.
And as a result of this spirit of urban
cooperation the plaza has become accessible to both the university and the
surrounding community.

Erol Akyavas photos

INDEX